Goin' On A Road Trip Without Any Wheels

Having the Adventure of a Lifetime for My Soul

Anna Greenlee

iUniverse, Inc.
New York   Bloomington

GOIN' ON A ROAD TRIP WITHOUT ANY WHEELS

Having the Adventure of a Lifetime for My Soul

Copyright © 2010 by Anna Greenlee

iUniverse books may be ordered through booksellers or by contacting:
iUniverse
1663 Liberty Drive
Bloomington, IN 47403
www.iuniverse.com
1-800-Authors (1-800-288-4677)

ISBN: 978-1-4502-2270-9 (pbk)
ISBN: 978-1-4502-2271-6 (ebk)
ISBN: 978-1-4502-2272-3 (hbk)

Printed in the United States of America
iUniverse rev. date: 5/19/10

Dedication

I want to dedicate this book to my wonderful family:
Jeff, Sarah and Colton.
Without them, simply put, there would be no book.
I am so grateful they let me be so honest.
Thank you for taking this life journey with me.
I love y'all.

I also want to thank our dog, Gracie for keeping my lap warm
all those hours I sat at the computer writing.

Thank you, Sarah for your designing creativity.

Colton would like for me to add a disclaimer.
When we lived in the camper, he was much younger than he is
now and no longer has to have his critters and blanket.
He has an image to protect.

Contents

Introduction

The summer of 2007, my husband decided to sell our travel trailer. It had been in the corner of the shop taking up room and collecting dust. Within just a few days, the trailer was gone. The twenty-eight foot fifth wheel may not reside in the Greenlee shop anymore, but it will forever be in my memory.

This was no ordinary vacation trailer to me. Sure, we took it on the typical family outings. We camped in it at lakes, state parks, big cities and even at my in-laws. But the majority of the trailer use came from living in it for nine (yes, nine) long months. Thus, the family's fondest camping memories came *not* from when we went somewhere, but when we went *nowhere.*

As I reflect back on living in the camper for that length of time, I find God revealing to me some great spiritual lessons that can be found between those four fiberglass walls—no traveling required.

God used camper life with my husband, Jeff, my two kids, Sarah and Colton, and a dog named Pooh to lead me on a spiritual road trip for the soul—one that ends in true joy and peace. All I have to pack is my Bible, and the only place I have to go is straight to Him.

Let the journey begin.

1

A New Adventure

Following God

"By faith Abraham, when called to go to a place he would later receive as his inheritance, obeyed and went, even though he did not know where he was going. By faith he made his home in the Promised Land like a stranger in a foreign country; he lived in tents, as did Isaac and Jacob, who were heirs with him of the same promise. For he was looking forward to the city with foundations, whose architect and builder is God."

Hebrews 11:8-10

By faith, our adventure in trailer living began with God placing a desire in our hearts to move from our Texas home west of the small town of Vega to a place closer to the big city of Amarillo. This wasn't an easy decision. We had a home we loved on eighty-five acres in the country. Our closest neighbors were my parents who lived a mile away. I liked to call it our *Little House on the Prairie.*

This house was the first home Jeff and I owned. We had, thus far, raised our children there from the time they came home as bundles of joy from the hospital. First words, first steps…this house was full of firsts for our children. Lots of memories.

Our house was quiet and peaceful, but it's location created a long and often tiring commute to work, ballet lessons, and dirt bike tracks, and (most important)our house wasn't where God wanted us. So we put our place up for sale and waited and waited for a year for a buyer.

During that time, Jeff and I were making plans for our move: what area did we want to live in, did we want to buy a home already built or build one ourselves? Decisions, decisions, decisions.

Jeff thought he would enjoy the process of contracting a new home, and I knew he was more than capable (he is so talented). We bought 3 acres in a subdivision and started the plans for our new home.

Now, where to live while we were building our house? Tent living like Abraham, Isaac, and Jacob really wasn't an option for me. We looked at apartment life, but that wasn't very appealing either. Jeff and I both had our fill of apartment living during our college days. Renting a house was a possibility, but the landlords all seemed to want at least a one year lease. I sure was hoping to be in our home before a year was up.

As I prayed about where to live, the travel trailer kept coming to mind. There was a "God's peace" to that idea. (*And the peace of God, which transcends all understanding, will guard your hearts and your minds in Christ Jesus.* Philippians 4:7) I knew living in the camper was something God placed on my heart; otherwise it wouldn't have been my idea. I'm not exactly the roughin' it kind of gal. Jeff had originally bought the trailer just to get me to go camping.

When we were young and so in love, we would go tent camping. It was the fact that we were young and so in love that we even survived putting the tent up. I called it the divorce tent because by the time we had all the sides of the tent up at the same time, we were hardly speaking to each other. Once the tent was up, we did enjoy being out in God's creation with one another. But as I grew older and we had been married longer, tent camping wasn't much fun. I would, however, agree to camp in a nice stylish camper with its own bed and bathroom. I could do that.

The travel trailer we had sounded adventurous, as they all do. Ours was the Cougar; although we wondered if the Cougar could outlast an adventure such as this. We enjoyed camping in it, but to live in it? Jeff just didn't see how that was going to work. After all, a 28 foot travel trailer comes out to approximately 224 square feet of living space for him, his loving wife, the two kids, the dog and the horse. Well, the horse wouldn't fit. She'd just have to live somewhere else.

I kept reassuring Jeff that living in the trailer would work best for us. God is practical. We already owned the trailer so we would save money, and we could be very flexible with our time. We would not be committed to a lease, and…I would be okay with this, really.

From the time we sold our house to the time we had to be out of it was two weeks. We didn't have much time to think about our decision. We just started moving forward in the process of packing and loading up the trailer with the essentials.

Our family quickly learned that one person's essentials are another person's boxed items. We carefully packed every nook and cranny of space with something of value to someone. Yes, space was at a premium, but I knew we had to pack the certain critters (stuffed animals) and books that gave my children a sense of security. After all, the motherly guilt was setting in that I was moving them from the home they loved—the only one they had known.

Even though I knew the move was something God wanted us to do, it didn't make it any easier. Am I the only one who ever feels this way? There have been times in my life when God calls me to do something and I follow in obedience, but there may be some tears along the way. This was one of those times.

The worst night in the trailer for me was the very first night. The trailer sat just a few feet from our prairie home. As I looked out of the little trailer window, I could see our former home sitting there. With memories flooding my mind and tears overflowing onto my face, I realized that to begin a new adventure we sometimes have to say goodbye to the old one. It was time to say goodbye.

I found my strength in God and my comfort in His word. I knew I must step out in faith to believe God and trust Him.

Romans 4:3 says, *"Abraham believed God, and it was credited to him as righteousness."* I did believe God! We were supposed to move, and move we did.

Just like Abraham, we all have a calling on our lives, and it is God's hope that we fulfill that calling. Whether we fulfill our calling or not depends on us. We have to want to follow God's direction for our lives. Sometimes that requires change, maybe even a move on our part, and a whole lot of faith.

In the Gospels, Jesus would simple state to people, *"Come, follow me."* Those who dropped everything and followed Him were never the same.

Jesus says the same thing to you and me today. Luke 9:23 reminds us, *"If anyone would come after me, he must deny himself and take up his cross daily and follow me."* Daily, we are to seek Him, lay down our own self interest, and follow the path He has for us. There are no guarantees as to what lies ahead; we trust God and let Him lead the way. Our part is to be obedient.

The apostle Paul wrote to the early church to give them guidance in their Christian walk. In 2 Thessalonians 1:11-12 he prayed this for Jesus' followers, *"That our God may count you worthy of his calling, and that by his power he may fulfill every good purpose of yours and every act prompted by your faith. We pray this so that the name of our Lord Jesus may be glorified in you and you in him, according to the grace of our God and the Lord Jesus Christ."* I can personalize the scripture and make it my own. When I pray this prayer like this, *"May God count me worthy of his calling, and that by his power he may fulfill every good purpose of mine and every act prompted by my faith. I pray this so that the name of my Lord Jesus may be glorified in me and me in him, according to the grace of my God and the Lord Jesus Christ,"* it gives me direction for life's journey.

As time goes by, few things stay the same. I get older, my kids start growing up, and the world can seem out of control, but I have one constant in everything, my God, the One I chose to follow years ago.

I may not always know where my journey may take me, but I do know this: whether I am living in a travel trailer or a home with a solid foundation, He is my anchor. I love how Hebrews 6:17-19 gives me this promise, *"Because God wanted to make the unchanging nature of his purpose very clear to the heirs of what was promised, he confirmed it with an oath. God did this so that, by two unchangeable things in which it is impossible for God to lie, we who have fled to take hold of the hope offered to us may be greatly encouraged. We have this hope as an anchor for the soul, firm and secure. It enters the inner sanctuary behind the curtain, where Jesus, who went before us, has entered on our behalf."*

The God of my salvation is trustworthy and true. I know He will be with me no matter where I call home. He is my steadfast anchor in an ever changing world.

2

Drawers 'r Overflowin'

A Fulfilling Life

*"May the God of hope fill you with all joy and peace
as you trust in him, so that you may overflow with hope
by the power of the Holy Spirit."*

Romans 15:13

When I say we had every nook and cranny of the trailer full, I mean it was overflowing with the Greenlee necessities. We had a closet that was about three feet long and eighteen inches deep. Below the closet were six drawers about fourteen inches wide and six inches deep. This space would accommodate our clothing for the next nine months. And as the matriarch of the family, I got to do most of the "fitting stuff" in the closet and drawers.

Each family member had to have some space. I asked Jeff, "What do you need?" He said, "Just throw me in a few t-shirts and jeans. That's all I need." I know he was trying to make things easy on me, but I knew he might need a few more clothing items like some socks, tightie-whities and shoes. Jeff is a firefighter with the Amarillo Fire Department so I didn't have to worry about work clothes. They were provided and usually stayed in his locker at work. He really was the easiest to pack for.

I did explain to Jeff, "While your needs are simple, mine are not." (A fact that must be true in a lot of marriages…just guessing.) I didn't want to show up to Bible study and church each week with the same attire. So my loving husband came up with a solution for my dilemma. (He is so sweet. I thank God every day for Jeff.) He built me huge clothing racks to put in my mother's garage. On those racks, I put enough clothes for all of us to transition through the seasons. Boxes could fit neatly under the racks for clothes that wouldn't hang and shoes. The clothing racks worked out great.

The kids and I would head out to my mom's house on Friday or Saturday. I would wash clothes, and the kids could stretch out and have some room to play. I would replenish my supply of clean clothes and trade different ones out so it wouldn't look like we were wearing the same thing every week.

My mother welcomed our weekly visits. She missed having us as her neighbors. Our dirty clothes were an anticipated sight to see coming up the sidewalk; just as they were when my brothers would show up from college with duffle bags stuffed full of dirty laundry. As the little sister, I have to say,

"I think my bag of dirty laundry was a better deal for mom because I washed my own clothes—they did not."

I would spend laundry day washing and ironing and folding. Once the process was complete, I packed it in the minivan to take to the trailer. Upon returning to the trailer, Jeff couldn't help but notice the appearance of more clothes coming back than when I left: a few more socks, an extra jacket, a pair of shoes. The accusation was hard to deny when I started putting items back into the drawers and the closet. Everything fit a little tighter. It is kind of like when you put on your favorite pair of jeans and they fit just a little snug. You blame the dryer for shrinking them. The problem with the drawers and closet was they weren't as breathable as an old pair of jeans.

The closet and drawers were overflowin'! The poor closet rod was pulling its weight. I don't know why I bothered to iron the clothes because by the time I got them into the van, out of the van, back into the camper, and then stuffed in the closet; they weren't at their best. Thank God for Downey Wrinkle Releaser. A fresh bottle could always be found on hand.

The drawers weren't as forgiving as the closet. I would cram as much as I could into the drawers and then quickly shut them. There! It was fine. They shut. The problem came when we would try to open a drawer. It would be so full; the pressure to get it open would throw the drawer off track. We could get what we needed out of the drawer, but when we would go to shut the drawer, it would just lay there in a sad, crooked state refusing to close. To get the drawer back on track, we would have to unload that drawer and the one below it (the bottom drawer would expand when space above it was open), pull the drawer completely out and try to realign it to glide smoothly on its tracks. This wasn't easy and usually required Jeff's expertise.

Jeff told me we couldn't keep going like this. I couldn't keep filling the drawers to overcapacity. They wouldn't last. They weren't made for that kind of abuse. I knew he was right and began to slim down the stockpile of socks, undies and pajamas. I tried to be careful not to overfill the drawers, but every now and then, I would sneak in an extra pair of socks and the unforgiving drawer would call me on it. I did, however, learn to realign my own drawers!

A simple life lesson can be learned in the overstuffed drawers. I have to be careful how I fill my life—physically, mentally and spiritually. I don't want my life to be so overflowing with stuff (good or bad) that I get myself off track. Just to have a life that is *full* is not necessarily *fulfilling*; it is HOW I fill my life that makes all the difference in the world.

Time is the same for everyone. We all get the same twenty-four hours in a day, the same seven days in a week, and the same 365 days in a year. We get to choose how we want to fill those days.

We desire to have a life that is full of purpose and meaning, not one that is just busy. There is a huge distinction between having a full life and having a life that is fulfilling. God reaches out to each one of us wanting to show us how to have the life that is full by His measure. And His fullness is guaranteed to leave you satisfied not over-stuffed.

There are certain areas of my life that I want full, to the abundance and overflowing. In John 10:10, Jesus said, *"I have come that they may have life, and have it to the full."* The New King James version says, *"….have it more abundantly."* That is the life I want. The one God has for me is fruitful and full of joy and peace.

But Satan, the prince of the world, always has other ideas for my life. Just as God has a plan for my life so does Satan. It's my choice to choose which path I want to follow. If you go back to the first part of John 10:10, it says, *"The thief comes only to steal and kill and destroy."* Satan is anything but honorable. He will do whatever it takes to keep me from having the life that Jesus wants me to have. Satan can fill our lives with the known bad things, but remember; he is tricky, and can fill our lives with things that seem harmless too. He will use anything to distract us from the best that God has prepared for us. He may have me feeling like my life is full, even so full it can be overwhelming.

If Satan keeps my life filled to the brim with the wrong things, there is no room to be filled with right things. My life becomes anything but abundant. I lose my joy, my hope, and my assurance of who I am. When that happens, I am not any good to anybody: as a wife, as a mother or as an ambassador for Christ. My life loses meaning and purpose. I become like the overflowing camper drawers. I am full, but off track in a sad, crooked state.

How do I find myself not living the abundant life Jesus describes in John 10:10? It's not hard. I can do it in a day, a week or gradually overtime.

Physically, I can overload myself with activities that may seem harmless, but if I haven't checked with God to see if that is how I need to be spending my time, instead of feeling fulfilled I just feel drained. If I am busy with the wrong activities, I may miss out on what God wants me to do, then I would miss a blessing (and I don't want to miss God's blessing). I have learned that it is okay to say, "No!" God is the one I answer to first. He is the perfect scheduler of my time.

Mentally, I really have to watch negative thoughts. Negative thoughts produce negative actions, and Satan always knows what buttons to push to get a response from me that is less than desirable. When you are a Christian and living with the Holy Spirit inside of you, these thoughts and actions quench the Holy Spirit, and they don't glorify God. Some of those thoughts can be anger, bitterness, greed, and unforgiveness. If I continue to dwell on such emotions, my mind becomes full of ideas that just bring me down. Then I'm asking myself, what has happened? This is an area that I am really working on. I have to take my thoughts captive and make them obedient to Christ. (2 Corinthians 10:5) Once I have taken the negative thoughts captive, I have to replace them with good, positive, Godly thoughts. I cling to Philippians 4:8-9, *"Finally, brothers, whatever is true, whatever is noble, whatever is right, whatever is pure, whatever is lovely, whatever is admirable—if anything is excellent or praiseworthy—think about such things. Whatever you have learned or received or heard from me, or seen in me—put it into practice. And the God of peace will be with you."*

Spiritually, there is only one place to go for true fulfillment. That is straight to my Lord, Jesus. He truly is the key to an abundant life. This becomes a heart issue. Do I love the Lord with all my heart, soul and strength? I have to routinely and honestly ask that question. I don't want someone or something else to take the top spot of God. If I do, that becomes idolatry. Our God is a jealous God (Exodus 34:14), and He expects to be first in my life. This is what God commands of all of us. Deuteronomy 6:4-6 says, *"Hear, O Israel: The LORD our God, the LORD is one. Love the LORD your God with all your heart and with all your soul and with all your strength. These commandments that I give you today are to be upon your hearts."*

If I keep God first in my life and spend time with Him first thing in the morning, emptying myself out to Him, asking Him to fill me with His Holy Spirit, the rest of my life seems to fall into place much better. I find my life overflowing with the things it is suppose to overflow with such as the fruits of the Spirit: *love, joy, peace, patience, kindness, goodness, faithfulness, gentleness and self-control.* (Galatians 5:22-23)

If you are living in God's will, you will find its okay to overflow in certain areas. In fact, it is scriptural. When I am living in the Spirit, I become more thankful and when I am more thankful, I find myself more generous to others in action and deed, and when I am more generous, I discover that I cannot out-bless God. My life has purpose and meaning. Luke 6:38 becomes a reality. *"Give and it will be given to you. A good measure, pressed down, shaken together and running over, will be poured into your lap. For with the measure you use, it will be measured to you."*

Through Jesus, God hopes to give us an abundant life so full of His love and grace that it just naturally spills over onto others. However; it is our choice how we live our lives.

God has given us free will. We can choose to have a life full by God's standards or we can try and fill it by the prince of this world's standards.

I don't know about you, but my desire is to have my life overflowin' the way it is supposed to be: with an overabundance of some Godly stuffin'. And I wouldn't want it any other way!

3

Privacy, Where?

Open Before God

"Nothing in all creation is hidden from God's sight.
Everything is uncovered and laid bare before the eyes of him
to whom we must give account."

Hebrews 4:13

The first few months of our adventure were spent at an RV resort. Sounds glamorous; doesn't it? "Resort" in RV talk must mean park between two trailers.

We weren't in the trailer long before we realized there wasn't much privacy to be found…anywhere. Being that we moved off of eighty-five acres, we were used to some breathing space. Our breathing space had turned from miles to inches. Anyone within just a few feet of the trailer could hear us, and we could hear them. I would be lulled to sleep at night by the sound of the diesel pick-ups pulling in. Ah, resort living.

There were privacy issues inside the trailer as well. It wasn't like you could go to your room and shut the door or go to the bathroom and take a nice hot bath. Nope, we were all right there together. Like it or not.

It didn't take long for me to notice that the lack of privacy within our family might bother me a bit. The whole privacy thing became very apparent when I was on the computer. (Jeff had fixed a spot for our computer and printer to fit in the camper so we could still have the use of it.) One evening, I was checking my email and right over my shoulder hovering to read every word were my daughter and our dog. I thought—this might be a problem.

To add to the joy of our close quarters, that spring at school my children were both introduced to recorders in music class. In my day, we called them flutaphones. Never mind what you want to call them, we not only had one, but two, to practice. And practice we did. For a few minutes each day after school, you could hear from our trailer the sounds of the Greenlee Jamboree. Our dog, Pooh, would even join in with some howlin' of her own, and who could blame her. It was the kind of music that made you want to howl! I spent that time praying no one would come to our door with a different idea about our music. Thank God no one ever did.

Sleeping time was an adjustment for all of us. Things had to shut down when it was time for the kids to go to bed. Their beds where made from the couch pulling out and the dining room table breaking down. They weren't the most comfortable beds around, but they served their purpose.

Sarah and Colton would argue over who got the couch (it was the fluffier of the two).

One night, I heard a huge thud and found Sarah had rolled off the bed. Another night, Sarah woke me up trying to sleepwalk out the front door. We could hear everything from each other's breathing, to snoring, to tosses to and fro. I don't think even a nose scratch went unnoticed.

Our dog even lost her privacy. Pooh's bed rested right under the couch so she learned her relaxing time of gnawing on a rawhide was unwelcome past a certain hour.

Jeff and I did have a sliding door that separated our bed from the rest of the trailer so we could stay up a little longer, but we had to be very quiet or the kids (well, Sarah) would let us know we were being too loud. Colton would never complain about us being too loud. I'm sure he was hoping he could hear something that might be used to his advantage later.

My morning routine included rising early to have my quiet time with God. When Jeff was at the fire station, I could stay in the bed and pray and have my study time there. But when he was home, I would spend that time in the bathroom. God really will meet with you anywhere. All He needs is an open heart, the place is irrelevant.

We learned to live with the lack of privacy. In fact, we got so used to being underfoot of one another that when we moved into our home; we found we had to have some snuggle time together in the recliner. (Jeff is pretty sure the kids and I are going to break the oversized chair someday, but it hasn't stopped us yet.) There was a sense of security, a special bonding we had in our lack of privacy.

Over time, our family learned that there was joy in our closeness without privacy. What at first seemed like a problem become a treasure.

The same is true in our relationship with God. As human beings, we may be intimidated, even bothered, at the thought of our Creator knowing everything about us. When I was a kid, this concept scared me to death. "He knows what I am thinking? I'm doomed to hell!!!" But as I matured in the Lord (thank goodness), I discovered great comfort, even relief in knowing He knows everything and still loves me. And because He knows everything, I know how much I need Him.

I love the words of David in Psalm 139:13-16, *"For you created my inmost being; you knit me together in my mother's womb. I praise you because I am fearfully and wonderfully made; your works are wonderful, I know that full well. My frame was not hidden from you when I was made in the secret place. When I was woven together in the depths of the earth, your eyes saw my unformed body. All the days ordained for me were written in your book before one of them came to be."*

Judging by David's words, our lives have never been private from God. No, He is the one who very personally took His hands and formed each one of us in the womb. He knew us then, and He knows us now, and He loves us. I find that amazing!

Our God isn't looking for privacy. We were created to fellowship with Him. He created a spirit inside each one of us that desires to be loved and in relationship with the Creator. That spirit inside us can only be satisfied by God alone. Even though He sees everything and knows everything about us, He wants us to come to Him and talk to Him about our lives, to lay it all before Him.

God longs for relationship with us, but since the fall of man in the garden with Adam and Eve, sin separates us from God. He is a pure and holy God and cannot enter into a relationship with us until a sacrifice is made for our sins. There has to be atonement for our impurity and unholiness. A blood sacrifice had to be provided for our iniquities so we could come before the Holy of Holies.

In the Old Testament, animal sacrifices were routinely offered for the atonement of sin. But God was prepared to provide a permanent sacrifice once and for all so we could have a relationship with Him while living in this fallen world. God had the perfect plan before the foundation of the earth for Jesus to be the unblemished sacrifice (1 Peter 1:20) for our sins. God sent His one and only son to die for our sins so that He could have a personal relationship with us. (John 3:16)

God doesn't want any privacy from His children nor does He want His children to think they should seek privacy away from Him. He wants an open door policy with us. That open door is Jesus. Jesus is our High Priest and sits at the right hand of the father as our intercessor. (Romans 8:34) I need Jesus. I need a savior. With Jesus as my High Priest, I know that I can apply Hebrews 4:16 and go boldly to the throne of grace that I may obtain mercy and find help in time of need.

I don't want privacy from God. He already knows everything anyway. He made me and understands me better than I understand myself. I desire a close relationship with Him, and the best way to do that is to be open and honest and keep the line of communication open.

There are benefits to going to God for a chat. He doesn't grow tired of listening to me, and when He speaks to me, He always has my best interest at heart. It is exciting too. The more I spend time with Him, the more I get to know God and His character.

It is comforting for me to know that I can bend the ear of the Creator of the universe at any time about anything, and He will lean down to listen with love to every word. Psalm 116:2 assures me of this. The New Living Translation says it like this, *"Because he bends down and listens, I will pray as long as I have breath!"* What an encouragement to pray! I'll say it again; I find God amazing.

In the New King James Version of the Bible, Jesus says in John 10:9, *"I am the door. If anyone enters by Me, he will be saved, and will go in and out and find pasture."* With Jesus as the door, we are always invited to walk right into the heavenly realms. You'll never find the sign, "Private, Keep Out!" hanging on God's door. And if we are wise, we will make sure it is a swinging door that allows God open access into our earthly realm where our hearts dwell. For our hearts can find rest in the presence of the Lord. *"Dear children, let us not love with words or tongue but with actions and in truth. This then is how we know that we belong to the truth, and how we set our hearts at rest in his presence whenever our hearts condemn us. For God is greater than our hearts, and he knows everything.*" 1 John 3:18-20

No privacy can be a good thing, especially when it is between us and our Creator.

4

Don't Blow a Fuse!

Anger Management

*"A fool gives full vent to his anger,
but a wise man keeps himself under control."*

Proverbs 29:11

Adjustments had to be made in our daily routines during trailer life. The Cougar was unforgiving towards what my family would call normal use of comforts from home.

We hadn't been in the trailer long when I discovered my excessive use of cooking appliances was not to be tolerated. One morning when cooking breakfast, I had the coffeemaker and the electric skillet going at the same time. That was enough to send the Cougar over the top and blow a fuse. Well, of all things! I learned that I couldn't have the toaster and the microwave operating at the same time either. Once again, the Cougar blew a fuse.

You would think anything with the name *Cougar* would be powerful enough to control a few electrical surges on it without getting huffy about it, but this cougar seemed to have some anger management issues. It couldn't stand the heat, but I was the one that had to learn how to stay in the kitchen.

The Cougar didn't leave the issues to just the kitchen. It had to drag its fuse issues to the bathroom. I was blow-drying my hair on high (how dare me), and yep, you guessed it. I caused another fuse to blow. After some experimenting, I figured out it was okay to blow-dry my hair if I kept the dryer on low. Unless you are a baby or a person with some thinning hair problems, it takes awhile for your hair to get dry when you can only use the low setting on the dryer. And I had three other people to share my bathroom space with! So I went to my hair stylist and told her I needed a short, trailer trash do! With a few giggles to go with the clip of the scissors, my stylist was happy to give me a shorter, faster-drying look to my hair.

Electrical currents weren't the only area of change we were forced to contend with. The camper came equipped with a stingy six gallon hot water tank. May I say, "I love hot water!" The hot water tank is a wonderful invention. To be able to turn on a handle at a moment's notice and have warm, soothing water flowing out of a faucet onto your fingertips is a blessing to behold, but the blessing can quickly turn to shock when the hot water suddenly turns rudely cold. The quick change in temperature comes all too soon with a miserly RV hot water tank.

The long leisurely showers and decadent bubble baths my family had grown accustomed to over the years were brought to a screeching halt. My husband showed us that we could only fill the bathtub just so full before the water would turn cold on us. (The kids called them stingy baths.) He also showed us that we couldn't turn the shower faucet on wide open; we would have to be happy with a softer flow of water coming down from the showerhead if we expected to finish the showering process with warm water.

I resented Jeff's hot water lessons a bit. In my defense, I felt I was at a bigger disadvantage in the bathing area. He and his thinning head of hair (Jeff is one of those that doesn't need a hairdryer) could get in and out of the shower with hot water to spare. I, on the other hand, had to lay hands on the hot water spigot praying for divine intervention so I could manage to get my hair washed, put the water on hold, shave my legs; and then, get all rinsed off with some amount of warm water coming out. It was an *I Love Lucy* moment every day.

During the trailer time, my son, Colton had to make some changes in *his* shower habits. He missed his long showers. Colton loves to take showers and feel clean. He takes showers twice a day like his mom. He'll stand under the water as it cascades down his body as if it is refreshing his whole being. For Colton, shower time had to go from being a soulful experience to being a time to wash the dirt off.

We hadn't been in the trailer very long, when Colton decided to go spend the weekend with his grandparents. While he was there, I got a call from my mother. She said, "I've got something funny to tell you." In the midst of her laughter she told me, "Colton has taken five showers in a day." I laughed too, but with a hint of jealousy.

We learned to make adjustments to appease the Cougar's temperament, but every now and then that temper of hers would rare-up and you guessed it…she'd blow a fuse.

I hate to admit it, but I can be like that cranky, old travel trailer. I'm fun and easy to get along with and will put up with quite a bit, but once I have had enough, I am very likely to blow a fuse of my own. And I must say (and God has showed me) that is not a very Christian way of dealing with issues.

The Bible has a lot to say about anger. First, I take comfort in the fact that the Bible says God is slow to anger. The Psalmist says in Psalm 86:15, *"You, O Lord, are a compassionate and gracious God, slow to anger, abounding in love and faithfulness."* Not only is God slow to anger, He doesn't keep hold of His anger, but is eager to forgive. I am eternally grateful for this fact. David writes of this in Psalm 103. He states, *"The LORD is compassionate and gracious, slow to anger, abounding in love. He will not always accuse, nor will he harbor his anger forever; he does not treat us as our sins deserve or repay us according to our iniquities. For as high as the heavens are above the earth, so great is his love for those who fear him; as far as the east is from the west, so far has he removed our transgressions from us."*

If God is slow to anger, and doesn't harbor His anger, and doesn't hold our sin against us; then as a Christian who wants to be an imitator of God, I should do the same. Ephesians 5:1 says, *"Be imitators of God as dearly loved children."*

The Bible not only offers scripture of how God handles anger, it also shows us how we should handle anger. Psalm 4:4 says this, *"In your anger do not sin; when you are on your beds, search your hearts and be silent."* Another verse worth noting is James 1:19-20, *"My dear brothers, take note of this: Everyone should be quick to listen, slow to speak and slow to become angry, for man's anger does not bring about the righteous life that God desires."* My husband always says, "There is a reason God gave us two ears and only one mouth. Maybe we should listen twice as much as we speak." Personally, I can't imagine why I have heard that more than once from him. Hmm. I don't think it is an original Jeff Greenlee quote, but it is a good one to remember.

God gives us some great words to live by on the subject of anger. Obviously, He knew anger would be something we would all have to deal with. So many people can make us angry on a daily basis. Certain issues or injustices can cause anger to rise within us. The question we have to ask ourselves is, "How do we learn to handle our anger?" We have to learn to hand our anger over to God.

It is imperative to remember that God is lovingly gracious and compassionate when he deals with *me*. I am not perfect, and when I mess up, He doesn't blow up at me. Therefore, I should extend the same loving grace to others.

Dealing with anger effectively is a mind process in which I am trying to acquire success. Notice I said trying. I need to take the time to first pray and remind myself about what

Jesus' love has done for me. He gave Himself up as a ransom to set me free from a bondage of sin (Hebrews 9:15). Oh, how He loves me. Hallelujah! Praise God! Dwelling on that thought diffuses my anger. Then I can ask God to help me in this situation. If I take the time to go through that thought process, then I am calmer to deal with the issue that needs to be dealt with in a Godly way. Plus, I have to remember God sees everything, and He is ultimately in control.

I really don't want to find myself reacting to anger in a way that is inappropriate. I can only do this so well in my own strength (okay, not well at all). I need the Holy Spirit's help. Believe me I know this lesson from experience.

Just the other day, I found myself saying something I never intended to say. I had even told myself, and others, I was going to keep my mouth shut over a certain situation. Notice, I keep saying I, not God—big mistake. Instead of going to God with this situation, every time this person did something to upset me, I just shoved it down inside me thinking I had a handle on things. Let me tell you, dealing with matters in my own strength just does not work. Finally, the person said something, and I was at my boiling point. Words spewed out of me that I had never planned to say. I couldn't believe I did that. It wasn't exactly a victorious moment in Christ. I repented, and thank goodness His mercies are new every morning. (Lamentations 3:23) But as my dad always says, "I've learned something new here."

I see the wisdom in Ephesians 4:26-27. Paul says, *"In your anger do not sin. Do not let the sun go down while you are still angry, and do not give the devil a foothold."* I have learned from experience that I need to take everything to God, no matter how small it may seem at the time and give it to Him. I can complain, tell him what is bothering me or what makes me angry and then leave it there with Him. He is ready to listen. He is the best counselor there is. By venting my frustrations to God, I don't let them build up inside of me giving Satan an opportunity to use that pent-up anger to blow a fuse at an unexpected time. Fuse blowing is not very Christ-like.

The Cougar will still blow a fuse if certain circuits are overloaded. I, however, hope that I can get to the point where the fuse just won't ignite. I pray the fuse that is in me will become so saturated with God's love and grace that I won't have any other choice but to let it die out.

5

Teaching an Old Dog New Tricks

A New Creation

"If anyone is in Christ, he is a new creation;
the old has gone, the new has come!"

2 Corinthians 5:17

Our little dog was a mutt we had gotten from an animal shelter. It was guestimated that she was a terrier mixed with only her momma knows. She was a cute and furry dog we grew to love.

We had gotten her when Colton was just a few months old, and Sarah was almost two. Jeff and I let Sarah name her. Sarah's world at the time consisted of *Cinderella, Sesame Street* and *The Adventures of Winnie the Pooh*. So going with what she knew, Sarah named our new dog Pooh. I'm sure Pooh Bear was honored to have the namesake.

Pooh loved our family and our country home. She loved going on walks and having free range of our place. I enjoyed having her around too. She was a good dog who never wandered off like the beagles we had before. (The beagles couldn't help themselves. Rabbit trails would call their names and off they would go until one day they would never return. We figured coyotes would get them and I would be broken-hearted.) We knew this time, we needed a different breed of dog; one that wouldn't wonder. I was thrilled that Pooh would always stay close to her home.

In the nine years Pooh lived in the country, she developed her routine. She would come in and out of the house as she pleased when we were home. When we were out for the day, she had a pen she stayed in with all the luxuries a dog needs. At night, she would sleep in her doghouse in the garage right by the door to the house. Pooh liked her resting spot there. She could quickly alert us if she felt anything was amiss. Pooh especially took great offense to owls trying to perch on our back porch during the night.

We were worried about our move into the trailer as far as Pooh was concerned. Pooh wasn't a puppy anymore. She was sixty-three in people years. That is, pretty set in your ways: old. She had always lived out in the country. She was used to horses and pasture. Pooh was not used to seeing strangers on a regular basis. We just didn't know if a country dog could take up with city living, but we were ready to find out. Pooh was part of the family, and she was coming along with us, and she was going to endure, I mean enjoy, this adventure along with the rest of us.

We put Pooh's comfy bed right by the couch and under the television. Our bedroom was just a step up from there.

She seemed okay with that. In fact, she liked being so close to all of us. In her doggie mind, I think, she thought she had upgraded to a 224 square foot doghouse.

Her new sleeping arrangements bothered us more than they bothered her (the privacy thing). She was always ready to go to bed when we were. She just wasn't prepared to stay retired. If she had trouble sleeping: she would get her rawhide and start gnawing with tireless intensity or she would get up and go get a drink of water. Have you ever noticed it is impossible for dogs to drink quietly? It just isn't in their DNA. In the best interest of man's best friend, we made sure the rawhides and water were put away every evening.

One thing she could never get over was the need to guard her family at ALL hours of the night. At the resort, we had a nice young man who lived beside us while he was going to college. As a lot of college kids do, he seemed to enjoy partying 'til the cows come home (which was about 2 a.m.) several nights a week. If it wasn't enough to hear his specially rigged Dodge diesel pick-up drive right by my head at that hour of the morning, we all got to hear Pooh announcing his arrival next door. She never could understand why we weren't always happy to receive her warnings of possible danger.

She was suspicious of all new people until she had a feel for them. Once she sensed they would cause us no harm, she would greet them with a sniff and a wag hoping the greeting would be reciprocated with a pat and a rub. However, there were a few neighbor kids she was snippy with. I couldn't blame her though; they made me a little snippy too.

Bless her little heart, Pooh was a trooper. She seemed to make the necessary adjustments with ease and grace. She never once had an accident in the camper. She waited for her walks around the RV resort. She didn't mind being tied to a harness for her walks. She was enthusiastic to explore new uncharted territory while attached to a fellow Greenlee. There was a sense of safety in exploring knowing she was connected to someone who was there to protect her and keep her from harm.

When left alone in the camper, Pooh did find herself in some mischief. She was good to not chew on anything she wasn't supposed to. Thank goodness she wasn't a puppy at the time or who knows what we would have come home to. She did, however, discover if she got up on the dining bench she could reach the trash can and knock it over. A feast was there to be had. We learned we had to put the trash out of her reach when we left. If we forgot, coffee grounds and remnants of a gorging would await us upon our return.

Our all-time favorite memory of Pooh took place in the camper. Every time we think of it, we can't help but break out in laughter. After we had moved the camper out to the building site, Pooh could go in and out of the camper at her will. She was good to stay on our land so we didn't worry about her.

One beautiful fall night, the kids and I were sitting in the trailer. We had just the screen door covering the entrance to the camper so we could enjoy some fresh night air. With her aging eyes, she looked up and saw an open door. But with the spirit of a puppy, she leaped up the steps expecting to dive right into the living area. Pooh's face met the screen door and she bounced off that thing like a gymnast bouncing off of a spring board. Poor thing, she didn't know what hit her. Being the supportive family members that we are, all we could do was laugh. She was fine, just a little confused and a lot more cautious when she entered through a door after that.

Pooh survived the trailer experience. In fact she did great. She adjusted and changed to her circumstances better than we thought she would. Pooh made the move into the new house with us. Her home was where her family was. That is all that really mattered to her.

With tears in my eyes, I have to say we had been in our home only six months when she died. We loved her and miss her. I will always remember her special time with us. Pooh showed me that you *can* teach an old dog new tricks.

If a dog is able to change and make adjustments in her life, then, as a Christian, how much more should I be able to make changes in my life to become more like Christ? I am to: *"put on the new self, which is being renewed in knowledge in the image of its Creator."* Colossians 3:10

As a born again believer, I have the Spirit of the Lord in me. And where the Spirit of the Lord is there is freedom. (2 Corinthians 3:17) Can I get an Amen!! Not only do I have freedom in Him, God gives me freedom to change my old self into a new creation. The good news is that I *can't* do it in my power. Nope, I fail every time I try to do it in my own strength. The power comes from the Holy Spirit.

If you're like me, there are many things I want to change about who I am. Maybe you're not like me and you have it all together. God Bless you.

Some of the things I have wanted to change have been small areas of my life that God has gradually revealed to me over time that need adjusting towards His glory.

He always seems to use Bible studies to work out those areas. That is why it is so important to be in some form of Bible study. My friend and fellow Bible study teacher, Tammy and I have always said, "We couldn't afford the amount of therapy we felt like we have had through Bible studies."

I keep my Bible studies I have taken through the years in a certain spot in my house. Tammy knows where they are; when I die, she is to come get them and burn them. I am to do the same for her. It's a pact we have had for years.

My studies have been a process of spiritual growth where I have laid my heart out to God. When you are so honest before God, you don't always want someone else reading your stuff.

Some honesty stuff (sins and hurts that have created some deep scars) have been things from my past that I can't really change, but I am not defeated by them nor do they define me. They are things I cannot change, but I can let Jesus redeem them. Jesus' redemption over me changes who I am. I am no longer the same person I use to be. I am free from my past.

The Holman Illustrated Bible Dictionary gives the definition of redeemed as such: "To pay a price in order to secure the release of something or someone. It connotes the idea of paying what is required in order to liberate from oppression, enslavement, or another type of binding obligation." [1]

Jesus came to this earth to redeem us from our pits of sin, despair, and hurts—whatever they may be. Only He has the ability to do this because He paid the price of death on the cross so that we can have freedom. We may not be able to go back and change our past, but Jesus can claim it for His glory. Satan is defeated by the blood of Jesus and the word of our testimony. (Revelation 12:11) Let Jesus have the victory.

One major key I have found to this liberty is to verbally confess what is on my mind. If it is sin…He can forgive it. If it is a hurt…He can heal it. If I cry out to my Jesus, Satan loses the power he has over me, and I find victory in Jesus. I then can praise my God saying Psalm 71:23, *"My lips will shout for joy when I sing praise to you—I, whom you have redeemed."*

I cannot stress how important this concept is to confess with your mouth what is on your mind. I used to think—well God knows it is there, and I know it is there—so I'll pray in my mind about this, and God will take care of it. But the truth was: I only found true freedom when I said what was on my mind out loud and that action opened my heart up for healing in that area. This exercise of faith breaks the chains Satan has on me.

That's why, when the Bible states in 2 Corinthians 3:17, *"Where the Spirit of the Lord is, there is freedom,"* God's perfect Word follows it up with verse 18. Because when a believer has found freedom in Christ, they love Him so much they want to be changed from the inside out. Take a look at what 2 Corinthians 3:18 declares, *"And we, who with unveiled faces all reflect the Lord's glory, are being transformed into his likeness with ever-increasing glory, which comes from the Lord, who is the Spirit."* The New King James Version says it like this, *"But we all, with unveiled face, beholding as in a mirror the glory of the Lord, are being transformed into the same image from glory to glory, just as by the Spirit of the Lord."*

This passage is so beautifully explained by the Biblical commentary of *Barnes' Notes* this way:

"The splendor, majesty, and holiness of God as manifested in the gospel, or of the Lord as incarnate. The idea is that God was clearly and distinctly seen in the gospel. There was no obscurity, no veil, as in the case of Moses. In the gospel they were permitted to look on the full splendor of the divine perfections-the justice, goodness, mercy, and benevolence of God-to see him as he is with undimmed and unveiled glory. The idea is, that the perfections of God shine forth with splendor and beauty in the gospel, and that we are permitted to look on them clearly and openly.

It is possible that there may be an allusion here to the effect which was produced by looking into an ancient mirror. Such mirrors were made of burnished metal, and the reflection from them would be intense. If a strong light were thrown on them, the rays would be cast by reflection on the face of him who looked on the mirror, and it would be strongly illuminated. And the idea may be, that the glory of God, the splendor of the divine perfections, was thrown on the gospel, so to speak like a bright light on a polished mirror; and that that glory was reflected from the gospel on him who contemplated it, so that he appeared to be transformed into the same image. Locke renders it: "We are changed into his very image by a continued succession of glory, as it were, streaming upon us from the Lord." The figure is one of great beauty; and the idea is, that by placing ourselves within the light of the gospel; by contemplating the glory that shines there, we become changed into the likeness of the same glory, and conformed to that which shines there with so much splendor."[2]

It truly is my heart's desire to be a reflection of Him. That is one of my ongoing goals in this lifetime. And I know it is a process I will be working on until the day I am in Glory and see My Savior face to face. For I know my citizenship is in heaven and I eagerly await my Jesus to transform this lowly body into a glorious body. (Philippians 3:20-21)

This side of heaven, God doesn't expect perfection from me or you. Thank God for His grace. He wants a relationship with us; and the more we spend time with Him in prayer and in His word, the more we begin to be more like Him in our thoughts and deeds. We can't help but change no matter how old we get! It is an ongoing process. So as Paul says in Philippians 2:12-13, *"Continue to work out (cultivate, carry out to the goal, and fully complete) your own salvation with reverence and awe and trembling (self-distrust, with serious caution, tenderness of conscience, watchfulness against temptation, timidly shrinking from whatever might offend God and discredit the name of Christ).[Not in your own strength] for it is God Who is all the while effectually at work in you [energizing and creating in you the power and desire], both to will and to work for His good pleasure and satisfaction and delight."* (verse from The Amplified Bible)

As a Christian, change comes with a purpose in mind: to become a reflection of His glory. May He continue to teach me some new things, no matter how old this girl may get.

6

Burnt Brussels Sprouts

An Aroma of Christ

*"For we are to God the aroma of Christ among those
who are being saved and those who are perishing."*

2 Corinthians 2:15

Daily cooking was a little different in the Cougar galley. The camper had a nice kitchen that was great for cooking up some hamburgers or hot dogs, but to cook normal meals day in and day out provided some challenges.

Jeff and I had said that we wanted to try and have our normal routine for meals—not to go eat out all the time. Colton says, "Mom, you cook like you're from the 1950's." It isn't meant to be a compliment. I'm certainly not a gourmet cook. I just try to make balanced meals with vegetables a part of the menu. I guess all those years of home economic classes have been ingrained in my brain.

Right off the bat, I noticed that I couldn't buy groceries like I used to. Back when I had a house, I would go to the store about every two weeks and stock up on food. I would even go to Sam's Club and buy the large quantities of stuff. No more would that do. I had to discover a new way to shop. I found out I had to go to the store about every other day so the food would actually be able to fit in the camper-size refrigerator.

With a few pots and pans and a crock pot and… without blowing a fuse, I would do my best to give my family the nice 1950's meals they loved (or not)!?! My kids would have been much happier with pizza, hamburgers and chicken nuggets every night. Even with the homemade meals, I thought we had plenty of fast food and our share of sandwiches too.

In the small space we had, it didn't matter what I cooked, the aroma of it filled the air. I had all kinds of air fresheners stuck around the trailer, but I just couldn't seem to keep that fresh linen smell wafting throughout our living area. Whatever the meal was for the day always seemed to win out over the scent of the day. Even now, when my kids smell a roast cooking, I'll get groans of "not again." I think it brings back too many memories of too many roasts in the camper.

My family will unanimously agree that the worst lingering smell we had in the trailer was the day I burnt the brussels sprouts. I know, you're thinking, "Who eats brussels sprouts?" Well…we do. Now you know why Colton thinks I am a throwback from the 1950's. I cook a lot of different vegetables and usually my family likes them (they just may not admit it around their friends).

This one particular day, I had put those little cabbages on the stove and then proceeded outside to do something. I lost track of time and you know how the story goes. I come back in to find the pan burnt up and brussels sprouts sizzling and stuck to the bottom. The smoke had set off the smoke alarm, and the smell was overwhelming. On a good day, the smell of brussels sprouts is—well… (may I be so bold to say) a little farty. So when they have been burnt to a crisp, they are just down-right ugly.

The aroma was everywhere! It was like skunk had met wet dog. To my horror the scent was even drifting outside. You could smell it a mile away. No amount of air freshener could knock out that fragrance. The scent weaved into every fiber of the trailer. You could smell it on the couch, on the bed linens, and to our dismay, on our clothes.

We tried our best to air it out by opening windows, but that night we went to sleep with the scent permeating our every inhale. I think the kids were voting for a hotel, but we stuck it out and were still living and breathing the next morning. We survived only to discover the smell was a part of us. We felt like it was on our skin and in our hair. The kids took showers to try and get some relief from the odor. Then it was time to get dressed. Their clothes reeked of burnt brussels sprouts. I sprayed them with some freshener and told them they would be fine. They weren't. They were mortified that I would send them to school in such conditions.

The situation didn't go unnoticed at school. The fragrance was a part of their persona. For that day, my kids were the aroma of burnt brussels sprouts. They couldn't deny it or be removed from it. It was part of who they were. Some kids thought it was funny, some empathized with them, and some were flat turned off by them.

My life as a Christian shouldn't be much different than a life engulfed with smelly brussels sprouts. I should be the aroma of Christ according to scripture. A definition of aroma is: to have a distinctive intangible quality.[3]

2 Corinthians 2:14-17 states, *"But thanks be to God, who always leads us in triumphal procession in Christ and through us spreads everywhere the fragrance of the knowledge of him. For we are to God the aroma of Christ among those who are being saved and those who are perishing. To the one we are the smell of death; to the other, the fragrance of life. And who is equal to such a task? Unlike so many, we do not peddle the word of God for profit. On the contrary, in Christ we speak before God with sincerity, like men sent from God."*

Where the NIV says, *"we are to God the aroma of Christ"*, I love how the King James Version says, *"we are to God a sweet savour of Christ."* Whether you relish over being a *"sweet savour or an aroma of Christ"* to God, I see that as ones who bear the name of Christ, we are smelly. We are either the fragrance of life to those who choose Christ or we are the smell of death to those who reject the message of Christ.

I tell you, 2 Corinthians 2:14-17 has some meat to it. It asks, *"Who is equal to such a task?"* Those who are sincere before God—those are the ones up for the task. That makes me go to my knees in prayer. I want to represent God well—as if I am on a mission straight from the throne seat of God. Oh, how I want to offer up my life to God as a "sweet offering" so He can use me. And can I add, "I don't want to embarrass Him." (I know God doesn't get embarrassed. He knows who He Is. I just don't want to be the cause of someone thinking badly of Him.)

You and I are to live a life that is offered as a sacrifice to God so that He can work in us and through us for His glory. Romans 12:1 says this, *"Therefore, I urge you, brothers, in view of God's mercy, to offer your bodies as living sacrifices, holy and pleasing to God — this is your spiritual act of worship."*

Under the Old Testament law, burnt offerings, offerings made by fire, were a pleasing aroma to the Lord. In the New Testament, Jesus became the ultimate offering to the Lord for our sins and this was pleasing to God. Ephesians 5:2 states, *"Christ loved us and gave himself up for us as a fragrant offering and sacrifice to God."* Jesus literally gave His life for mine in the shedding of His blood on the cross so that I can have eternal life. Accepting Jesus' gift of salvation, I should sincerely offer up my life to be used as an act of worship to the Lord. This type of offering can be done in a variety of ways.

One way is to simply be kind to others—to be gracious to people we see in our daily lives from the postman, to the waitress in the restaurant, to the cashier at the grocery store. A smile and a kind word go a long way to share the love of Jesus in this world.

Although, this action might give you a response you aren't exactly expecting. One day I ran into the store while Jeff and the kids waited in the car. We had gotten back from a trip, and I just needed a few things before we went home.

I set my items down on the conveyor belt and smiled at the young cashier and asked, "How are you doing." He looked up at me and said, "Fine, how are you." We exchanged a few pleasantries and then he said, "You have a beautiful smile." I said, "Thank you." And then He said, "You must have been a real heartbreaker in *your* day." I had just had a birthday and was well aware I wasn't a spring chicken anymore, but I wasn't ready to hear the term "in your day" either. I got so tickled—it was all I could do not to start laughing so I had this silly grin on my face trying to contain myself. The young man had a pleased look on his face thinking he had just made my day with that comment. When I got to the car, I told Jeff the "compliment" I had just received and Jeff's response was, "Oh dear, I bet that went over well." All I can say is that God has a sense of humor!

Another way to be an offering to the Lord is to be ready to let the Holy Spirit prompt you to be a blessing to those in need. I love to send cards. (When I was in high school, I entertained the idea of having a Hallmark store when I grew up.) So I send cards to people that God places on my heart. Sometimes He will keep bringing someone to my mind that might need a phone call and an encouraging word. I've even had God place someone on my heart that might need some money. We just need to be in tune to the Holy Spirit so that he can prompt us towards a love gesture when needed.

Our testimonies are also a powerful way to share God's love with others. Our story of when Jesus came into our lives is a declaration of our faith. People need to hear that God can do amazing things in their lives. They need to know there is hope. No one is beyond being saved by the grace of God—no one. We need to be ready to share with others the joy we have in knowing Christ as our Savior. *"Always be prepared to give an answer to everyone who asks you to give the reason for the hope that you have."* This scripture comes from 1 Peter 3:15. We can know that our mistakes and failures that have been redeemed by Christ have not been in vain. We can share our redemption story with others to help spread the gospel of Jesus Christ. What an honor to be a part of God's divine plan—to know that what Satan meant for evil God meant for good. (Genesis 50:20) I hope I take every opportunity to share with others what God has done in my life so that I may bring glory to the One who knows I would be lost without Him.

These kinds of offerings allow the Holy Spirit to open the door for Christians to share the gospel with others. I think this is a pleasing aroma to our Maker. When this happens, we are different from the lost world—we are a distinct aroma of Christ. We have a purpose in life, one that is greater than ourselves. The world is screaming, "It's all about me!" We need to be sharing, "It's all about Jesus!" When we share the gospel with others, it is up to them to receive the message. Because of each person's free will; some will choose to accept the sweet perfume of eternal heaven, while others will choose the stench of hell. The choice is theirs.

My prayer is that I will have a sweet, distinct, intangible fragrance that will make someone ask, "What is it about you that seems different?" And I can say, "It's Jesus." He's the most valuable perfume we can wear. The scent is priceless, simply priceless.

7

Stormy Weather

Peace in Troubled Times

"You have been a refuge for the poor,
a refuge for the needy in his distress,
a shelter from the storm and a shade from the heat."

Isaiah 25:4

There is a saying in the Texas Panhandle, "If you don't like the weather we're having just wait a few minutes…it'll change." We experience a variety of weather in our neck of the woods. (I guess I can't really say "woods" since we don't have any, so in our "vast prairie" would be more appropriate.) And I must mention the wind blows—spring, summer, winter and fall—the wind blows.

Jeff and I thought since we moved into the camper at the end of February that we had seen the worst of the winter weather, and we would be moving into springtime in the trailer. Boy, were we wrong. As I sit here writing today, it is March 3rd and we have snow on the ground and school was delayed because of blizzard-like conditions. The wind is blowing between 40 to 50 mph out of the north. Did I mention the wind blows here? Just the day before, it was sunny and "the wind" was out of the southwest with a temperature of almost 70 degrees. Go figure.

Our weather days in the travel trailer weren't much different. We started out with pretty decent weather. Jeff was busy arranging to have a man get started on the dirt work for the foundation of the house. While he was doing that, the kids and I were trying to think of some fun things to do around Amarillo for spring break. Most of the activities we came up with seemed to include being outdoors like going to Palo Duro Canyon and enjoying nature's beauty there.

Spring break plans quickly changed as we watched the snow start to fall and fall and fall outside our little camper window. On the 15th and 16th of March 2005, we got a grand total of 13.8 inches of snow to be followed up by another 4 to 6 inches of snow on the 26th and 27th.[4] Spring fever plans gave way to spring shiver plans. We found entertainment in bowling alleys and movie theatres, and of course playing in the snow. I don't know of any kid that can resist building a snowman or throwing a few snowballs even if they had planned on riding bikes and hiking trails.

The snow continued. On May 2nd we had 4.7 inches of snow.[5] It was the first recorded snowfall for that day in the Amarillo area. I was starting to tire of the white stuff, but as spring went on, we finally went from watching the snow fall to watching the rain fall. It was a "better than most" year for moisture which made the farmers happy but delayed the building process considerably. The rain also kept camper fever kiddos stuck indoors. You might say things were a little stressful in our cozy quarters. Being inside and knowing things weren't getting done on the house outside meant we would be stuck in the camper that much longer. My optimistic hopes of staying in the Cougar for about four months were diminishing.

After all the weather delays, the house building resumed and progress was made. The water well and septic tank were ready to go the first part of June, so we were able to say goodbye to resort living and hello to community living. We packed up our trailer and moved to Prairie West Estates. (For some reason, I hear the theme song to *The Beverly Hillbillies* in my mind. I may be hearing the theme song, but I am pretty sure my neighbors were thinking *The Beverly Hillbillies* when they saw us pull the rig onto our lot. Bless their hearts.)

Now June in Texas means severe weather. Heavy thunderstorms with hail and tornadoes are possible. Knowing that tornadoes are likely in the Panhandle, we were building a safe room in our house. In the event a tornado came our way, we could quickly take safe cover. We may have a safe room in our house, but there was no such thing in a fiberglass hull known as our home on wheels. Obviously, we had already made it through high winds rocking us to sleep, cold snow drifting at the door and rain pelting the window panes. But we hadn't faced a fierce tornado or severe hail storm, not yet, anyway.

The house was framed when we moved out to the place and the safe room was built, but the door was not securely attached to it so it wasn't *really* safe at that point. It still needed to have the finishing touches put on it. This detail did not go unnoticed by my children, especially Sarah, who is terrified of bad storms. Sarah would worry anytime she saw a cloud building. She would ask, "What will we do if a tornado comes our way." I told her, "Don't worry. When we lived in our old house, we only had to take shelter a few times in thirteen years. The odds of us having to deal with a tornado while we are in the trailer are slim."

For June of 2005, the weather records show the Texas Panhandle had ten tornadoes touch down.[6] Those facts don't include all the funnel clouds that came teasingly over. Ten tornadoes are ten too many. The meteorologists were busy that month keeping us up to date with the latest severe weather, and we were busy listening to their updates.

As life would have it, the severe weather didn't miss Bushland, Texas. We had only been on our lot with the trailer for about a week when, one evening, an ugly storm started heading in our direction. It had all the signs of doing some nasty damage. The eerie looking clouds coming our way contained hail and a funnel cloud that could touch down at any moment. The sirens in Bushland went off for people to take cover, and my kid's sirens went off in hysteria. To be honest, I was a little nervous myself. What were we to do? A trailer is not where you need to be in a tornado. We decided we would bundle up and go to the safe room. It was better than nothing.

The phone rang. The neighbor across the street called; she invited us to come over and wait the storm out with her family in their basement. What an answer to prayer! I'm surprised she could hear me on her end of the phone with Sarah and Colton crying and screaming in the background,

"We're gonna die!", but I made sure she heard, "We'll be right there."

My kids quickly gathered up necessities they thought they had to have. They latched onto a few of their favorite stuffed animals and their blankets and their Bibles (that made their momma proud). We started out the door and Sarah said, "What about Pooh. Isn't she coming?" I told her, "The neighbor didn't say we could bring Pooh, and she isn't a dog person. The neighbors don't have any pets at their house." That almost stopped the whole procession right there. The kids weren't going to leave without their dog. More hysteria! "We can't leave her here to die," they wailed. So Jeff, my man in shining armor, agreed to valiantly stay with the dog. He assured me that if the tornado touched down that he would be right over to take cover with Pooh in hand.

Reluctantly, the kids left Pooh, and we ran next door in the wind and pouring rain to find safe shelter from the storm. What a way to get to know the neighbors! The kids were still crying. They were scared of the storm and upset that they left Pooh behind. I kept hearing, "Pooh's gonna die!" They were upset Dad had stayed in the trailer too; they just felt like they were responsible for Pooh and needed to take care of her.

As our drama was playing out, our neighbor took us to the basement where her little kids were. The neighbor kids were playing and having a good time. Mine were not. Thankfully, we were in a Christian home, and they were so nice to open it up to us. We prayed, and I read some Scripture out of one of the Bibles we had. I am grateful that my kids knew to turn to God in their time of great need. They found peace and solace in the midst of a huge storm. Their faith and my hugs saw them through. I know as they get older, I won't always be there to put my arms around them and hold them through a storm. But God will always be with them, and their faith will see them through any storm of life.

We were in the basement for several hours waiting for the storms to pass. Praise the Lord, a tornado never did touch down and the hail was minimal. God had protected us. When we felt it was safe, we packed up the Bibles and the stuffed animals and the blankets and crossed the street to our home. Pooh and the rest of us were safe. It had been a long evening to remember.

I have to say, after the tornado episode, the rest of the weather we had while in the camper seemed pretty uneventful. Hallelujah! While storms slowed down here, we continued to watch on TV weather cause mayhem across the world. In August of 2005, we saw the United States face a huge storm. Hurricane Katrina hit the southern coastline hard. Like the rest of the country, we couldn't believe the devastation left behind.

We set our eyes on people who had no place to live. They had lost everything. I told my kids, "There are some people who would love to have a trailer like ours right now. They don't have a place to call home, not even a little travel trailer." Seeing the victims of Hurricane Katrina made my family realize just how blessed we were…we are.

I know rain falls on the righteous and unrighteous alike. We all will have our share of storms. It is how we deal with them and who we turn to in those storms that can make all the difference.

God didn't promise us that we would never see storms in our lives. In fact, Scripture says just the opposite. In John 16:33, Jesus tells His disciples, *"In this world you will have trouble. But take heart! I have overcome the world."* The Amplified Bible says it like this, *"In the world you have tribulation and trials and distress and frustration; but be of good cheer [take courage; be confident, certain, undaunted]! For I have overcome the world. [I have deprived it of power to harm you and have conquered it for you.]"* Can I hear an amen!?!

When I face the storms of this life, I can stand courageously knowing that I have a Savior who has already defeated Satan and his schemes over two thousand years ago. The worldly troubles that come my way, however bad they may seem, are only very temporary when I look at them from an eternal perspective. Because of Jesus, I know the battle has been won and I have the victory. I am a conqueror. In fact, I am more than a conqueror because I know nothing will separate me from the love of God (Romans 8:37-39). I have confidence in knowing there is a higher power over my problem, and He gives me the authority to stand against the schemes of Satan. I am empowered with the armor of God (Ephesians 6:10-18) to fight the good fight. I take out the sword (the Bible) and I start praying Scripture that pertains to my circumstances.

Looking at my trials from an eternal perspective not only empowers me, but it gives me peace. In John 16:33, when Jesus talks about overcoming the world, right before that He says, *"In me you may have peace."* I need peace in this crazy world. I get that peace from trusting in God—putting my faith in Him. It scares me to think where I would be without Him. If I didn't have Jesus, the storms of this life would toss me to and fro, leaving me hopeless and with little peace in this existence. My faith is everything to me.

The faith I have builds a trust in God during a storm and that trust gives me hope. James 1:2-4 says, *"Consider it pure joy, my brothers, whenever you face trials of many kinds, because you know that the testing of your faith develops perseverance. Perseverance must finish its work so that you may be mature and complete, not lacking anything."* 1 Peter 4:12-14 offers this encouragement, *"Dear friends, do not be surprised at the painful trial you are suffering, as though something strange were happening to you. But rejoice that you participate in the sufferings of Christ, so that you may be overjoyed when his glory is revealed."*

What good is our faith if it is never tested? I believe trials will test what we really believe, and those trials can bring us closer to God if we have the faith to trust Him completely with our situations. He always has a purpose and a reason for our trials. We may not understand them this side of heaven, but one day His glory will be revealed. I promise you that.

We can even learn to rejoice in the worst of circumstances because of God's promises of the inheritance we have waiting for us. I stand on the claims of 1 Peter 1:3-7, *"Praise be to the God and Father of our Lord Jesus Christ! In his great mercy he has given us new birth into a living hope through the resurrection of Jesus Christ from the dead, and into an inheritance that can never perish, spoil or fade — kept in heaven for you, who through faith are shielded by God's power until the coming of the salvation that is ready to be revealed in the last time. In this you greatly rejoice, though now for a little while you may have had to suffer grief in all kinds of trials."* This life as we know it is only temporary, so are our problems. We can rejoice in the midst of pain knowing we are children of The King whose kingdom will never go away.

I am so glad I do not have to face the storms of life alone. God gives me His word to empower me, He gives me His peace to permeate my being, and He gives me hope in knowing He is working on my behalf. What am I to do? I am to praise the Lord. With all that is within me let me praise his holy name (Psalm 130). I think it is imperative to praise God in the storms—to worship Him. The singing group Casting Crowns even has a song out called *Praise You in This Storm*.

Our God inhabits praise, and demons shutter when we praise the name of Jesus. There is **power in praise** especially when we don't feel like praising. When I praise, it brings me closer to God and my God becomes bigger and my problems become smaller; and I know in my soul everything is going to be all right. Praise you Jesus.

We all face trials. But as a Christian, I have an advantage because I know it is not in vain. My heart breaks when I read about horrible tragedies of this world or see the news of destruction on television. I also am aware of the lost and hurting people just going through the existence of life. I tell my kids all the time, "They need Jesus." The hopeless need the hope of Jesus.

I don't have all the answers to explain the trials we face this side of heaven: why a friend of mine lost her husband to cancer at the age of 46 after we prayed and believed him to be healed, or why brand new parents discover that their precious child God brought into this world has Down's syndrome, or why a wonderful lady I love and admire has suffered from multiple sclerosis for such a long time. I don't know, but I am sure, in His great sovereignty, God knows why he allowed such things. And in these circumstances, God can be glorified by the ones that have been through them when they reach out to others with love and grace saying, "I know how you feel. I've been there myself. Let me share with you how God has gotten me through it." I am inspired by listening to the stories of people who give God glory and praise for seeing them through the tough times.

2 Corinthians 1:3-4 gives us this promise, *"Praise be to the God and Father of our Lord Jesus Christ, the Father of compassion and the God of all comfort, who comforts us in all our troubles, so that we can comfort those in any trouble with the comfort we ourselves have received from God."* So our suffering is not in vain nor does God leave us to suffer alone. The God of compassion is always there in *all* our troubles.

In my faith, I am sure of what I hope for and certain of what I do not see (Hebrews 11:1). I know that God can use everything for His glory if we allow Him to mature us and use us. Romans 8:28 gives us that promise. *"And we know that in all things God works for the good of those who love him, who have been called according to his purpose."* Notice the verse didn't say, "…in some things or a few things." No, it said, *"…in all things."*

This life can be hard, but this life isn't all there is. Don't you want to tell others we have an inheritance that will never perish? These trials are just temporary. And not only will we weather these storms, we will have victory over the storms. Oh, how I want to share the hope of my existence.

When I see storm clouds gathering around me, the first thing I do is pray that those clouds will dissipate and the storm never even develops. I continue to praise Him. I study God's word and anticipate the miraculous. I believe the same God of Abraham, Isaac and Jacob is my God too. I know He is more than capable of giving me a miracle. I've seen it, and I believe it with all my heart. So I pray and praise. I pray the storm will be blown away and the Son will emerge gloriously.

If my prayers aren't answered the way I have anticipated, I still keep praying and praising believing that God is allowing the storm so that He may be glorified in it. Remember the two P's—prayer and praise. They are vital to a victorious life.

Have you ever just sat and watched a thunderstorm and saw the beauty and power in it? I'll never forget a stormy night several years ago. Jeff was at the fire station and a storm awoke me. I got up and looked outside our bedroom window. I decided to take a seat in the chair and watch with wonder. I saw God's greatness in the storm. The thunder would announce His presence and the lightning would strike down by the command of His hand.

During the storm, I sat and talked with God; and He would answer me with His voice of thunder. My soul was rejuvenated with fresh living water like a dry cracking ground is renewed from the heavenly storehouses of rain. It was an amazing experience to converse with God in the middle of the storm.

He is always near, especially through our scariest and toughest of storms, never forgetting His purpose. And we can be forever changed by the storm if we keep our eyes on

God. We can come out of the storm as a stronger and more mature Christian—one that God is able to use in greater ways than if we had never gone through the storm. To God be the glory.

The key is to trust God. His ways are perfect. The Lord declares, *"As the heavens are higher than the earth, so are my ways higher than your ways and my thoughts than your thoughts."* Isaiah 55:9

It may not be until I get to heaven that I understand all of the ways of God, but I know my faith allows me to say it is okay if I don't understand everything. I tell my kids all the time, "If we had all the answers to all our questions, there would be no need for faith; and without faith, it is impossible to please God." (Hebrews 11:6)

So I will choose to praise my Lord, the Maker of heaven and earth, whatever my circumstance. My soul will sing as the Psalmist sang Psalm 135:5-7, *"I know that the LORD is great, that our Lord is greater than all gods. The LORD does whatever pleases him, in the heavens and on the earth, in the seas and all their depths. He makes clouds rise from the ends of the earth; he sends lightning with the rain and brings out the wind from his storehouses."*

After reading Psalm 135, my soul is dancing. How great is our God! My feet just may have to join in with my soul and do a little dancing too. It's okay; no one is here but my little weenie dog, Gracie, and me. She is used to it. Sometimes she can't resist doin' a little praisin' jig herself. Let all creation praise His holy name. Rain or shine I will choose to praise you, Jesus. I just love Him so! And the good news is that He loves me and Gracie too.

I want to end this chapter with the words to my all time favorite hymn. I come from a line of praisers. We may not be able to sing, but it never stopped my family (just ask our poor spouses) from praising the Lord with our voices. For as long as I can remember (as a teenager it was so uncool); I would wake up to hymns blasted from our 1960's hi-fi stereo by my mother, who would play scratchy records of praise over and over again. The collection was full of artists like Jim Reeves, Elvis Presley, Red Foley, and my mothers favorite, Tennessee Ernie Ford (bless his pea pickin' heart). The words of those songs are ingrained in my mind.

Anytime I hear one of those faithful hymns, my heart is overcome with a presence of the Lord. The words etched in my memory make me aware that He has been with me through all the storms of this life. He has never left me nor forsaken me. When I hear one of the old familiar hymns, the words stir my soul and I think the Spirit of the Lord is just going to take me out right then and there.

I love all kinds of praise music, but when I hear the songs like *Amazing Grace, In the Garden,* or *The Old Rugged Cross,* I can hardly speak. However, nothing moves me as much as *How Great Thou Art.* I can't even describe the feelings that overcome me when it is played at church. It is a moment between me and God that is so precious I can't even put it into words. Someday when God takes me home, I hope it is at a time when I am just singing this song. What a way to go.

How Great Thou Art was written in Sweden in 1885 by Carl Gustav Boberg at the age of 25. The words came to him while he was walking two miles home in a thunderstorm from a revival at church.

I copied all four verses down because I think they are so beautiful. If you grew up in a traditional church like I did, you can appreciate the fact that all four verses are recognized; for when we sang a hymn in my church, the third verse always seemed to be left out, or if we were running late and one of the ladies' roast might burn, we would hurry things along by singing only verses one and four. Why is that? Maybe, when we get to heaven some of our time will be spent singing the overlooked verses to all our beloved hymns.

I pray that you will slowly read the beauty of these words and let them permeate your being. Soak them in, and when you find a storm cloud has gathered over you, you can remember these words that describe the awesomeness of our God and you can sing with all your heart, "My God, how great Thou art!"

> O Lord my God, When I in awesome wonder,
> Consider all the worlds Thy Hands have made;
> I see the stars, I hear the rolling thunder,
> Thy power throughout the universe displayed.
>
> Then sings my soul, My Saviour God, to Thee,
> How great Thou art, How great Thou art.
> Then sings my soul, My Saviour God, to Thee,
> How great Thou art, How great Thou art!
>
> When through the woods, and forest glades I wander,
> And hear the birds sing sweetly in the trees.
> When I look down, from lofty mountain grandeur
> And see the brook, and feel the gentle breeze.
>
> Then sings my soul, My Saviour God, to Thee,
> How great Thou art, How great Thou art.

Then sings my soul, My Saviour God, to Thee,
How great Thou art, How great Thou art!

And when I think, that God, His Son not sparing;
Sent Him to die, I scarce can take it in;
That on the Cross, my burden gladly bearing,
He bled and died to take away my sin.

Then sings my soul, My Saviour God, to Thee,
How great Thou art, How great Thou art.
Then sings my soul, My Saviour God, to Thee,
How great Thou art, How great Thou art!

When Christ shall come, with shout of acclamation,
And take me home, what joy shall fill my heart.
Then I shall bow, in humble adoration,
And then proclaim: "My God, how great Thou art!"

Then sings my soul, My Saviour God, to Thee,
How great Thou art, How great Thou art.
Then sings my soul, My Saviour God, to Thee,
How great Thou art, How great Thou art![7]

8
Love Thy Neighbor

Called to Love

"Jesus replied: 'Love the Lord your God with all your heart and with all your soul and with all your mind.' This is the first and greatest commandment. And the second is like it: 'Love your neighbor as yourself.' All the Law and the Prophets hang on these two commandments.'"

Matthew 22:37-40

For the most part, I like camping folk. Whenever we have traveled with our trailer, we have met some really nice people at the RV parks.

I'll never forget the first trip we took with the travel trailer. We went to San Antonio and then on to Corpus Christi. In San Antonio, we stayed at a very nice resort by RV standards (though not exactly out of *The Lifestyle of the*

Rich and Famous). It had an enticing pool that the kids could not wait to try out.

While Jeff was getting the trailer stabilized and level, the kids and I went to the cement pond. We unloaded all the beach towels and swim toys, and I took a nice chair under an umbrella and got comfy to read a book. I hadn't paid attention that I had nested right by a pay phone.

Shortly after our arrival, a lady came up to use the phone. I couldn't help overhearing her. (I really couldn't. She was right there, and I am a little nosey.) She was telling someone on the other end about her stay. This lady was excited to share that she was living at a resort where people from all over the world came to stay. Really? All over the world. Hmm. Now, I know San Antonio is a big tourist spot for people from other countries. I have seen them around, but not pulling big rigs into the RV parks. Were we staying at the same place? I got tickled at the lady, trying so hard to impress the person she was talking to. She was telling her that neighbors were exotic guests from who-knows-where coming and going. I guess it did sound better than saying, "There is a lady and her two kids at the pool from Vega, Texas." It just doesn't have the same ring to it, does it?

When we started living at the RV resort those first few months of house building, I joked with Jeff, "I am anticipating seeing guests from all over the world." In reality, we didn't see a bunch of foreigners, but we did see people from all walks of life come and go. Some were old; some were young. Some appeared to be wealthy with their big shiny busses, and some of more modest means came in their little trailers. Some were there because the hospital district was close, and they were staying while they got treatment. Some were staying there while they did contract work in the area. Some were going to college. Some had staked a claim and were living there—tired of paying property taxes. And some were staying there while their house was being built. (I don't know who would do that, really. What were they thinking?) We saw a little bit of everything, and for the most part everyone was nice and friendly. They were neighborly so to speak.

Then one day, a big rig pulled into our little corner of the world and turned it upside down. They weren't exactly from a foreign country: just Houston. These new neighbors were a large man and a pretty young lady with him. They were selling satellite dishes in the area and would be staying awhile. Their lifestyle wasn't the same as most of us in the resort. The music was loud and language could be heard from that area that made me want to cover my children's ears. Not to mention, questionable looking men would come around at all hours of the night to hang out at this particular site.

I was concerned because Jeff was at the fire station on many nights. That left me and the kids home alone, and I would have to walk Pooh in the evenings before we went to bed. The owner of the place watched over everything very carefully, but in the evenings and on Sundays, he usually wasn't around.

On one of those days that Jeff was at the fire station, I found myself in an unusual circumstance. It was a foggy, cold Sunday afternoon, and I was taking Pooh for our usual walk around the grounds. As I came upon the Houston trailer, the man opened the door and threw a large trash bag full of clothes out on the grass. Right behind the clothes came the beautiful young lady with eyes full of tears and mascara streaming down her face.

Immediately, Pooh and I were thrown into a situation we weren't exactly looking for. The lady looked up at me and asked if I had a phone she could use. I told her there was a cell phone in my trailer, and she was welcome to it. We grabbed her trash bag of belongings and headed to my home.

When I opened the door to our trailer, the kid's eyes got as big as saucers when they saw what was coming through the narrow opening. Sarah and Colton were in such shock that they were speechless—which was a good thing. I introduced my family to this girl and offered her a chair at the dining table and gave her my phone to use.

She called a friend of hers whose mother lived in Amarillo. She told me that the friend's mother would come get her and asked if it was okay to wait there until this lady came. I told her it was fine as I handed her a box of tissues.

While wiping away her tears, she started opening up about her situation. At the young age of nineteen, she had left a baby back in Houston with her mother so she could go with this man across the country. She said she was living with him because he had lots of money and could give her things she could never afford on her own, but with that came a hot temper and abuse. To add to that, she was pregnant with his child. She felt trapped in a situation with no way out.

My Bible was sitting on the table and I asked her if she knew Jesus. She said she did, but it had been a long time since He had been a part of her life. I told her, "He is always ready to have one come back home that has strayed, and He will accept them right where they are if they'll just turn to Him and say, 'Jesus I need you as my savior. Please forgive me of my sins.'" I read her some scripture and she listened.

We talked while my kids stayed uncomfortably busy watching a movie and playing on the computer. They were trying to act busy, but I could tell they were absorbing everything that was going on.

An hour went by . . . then two. I asked her if that friend's mother was coming to get her, and she assured me she was. I shared with her that there were organizations in Amarillo that help abused women, and I could get her to a safe house that day. She didn't want to do that and got upset when I mentioned it. "Okay," I said, "you can wait here until the lady comes for you." And wait we did.

A scary guy came to my door and wanted to talk to her. She went out and talked with him. She came in and told me he would give her a place to stay; although, he wanted "favors" and she wasn't willing to do that. I went out and asked him to leave and not come back. Then the man she was living with came over. He wanted to talk to her, and I had to ask him to leave.

I was getting a little nervous thinking about what I had gotten myself and my kids into. It was very cold outside, and I couldn't kick a young pregnant girl out the door. I just prayed for God to help me because I was out of my element.

Four hours later, the friend's mother finally showed up and took the girl with her. I reminded her of our conversation about Jesus and gave her the numbers of the organizations that could help her get out of this situation.

I tried to show the love of God to the girl on that day. I have often wondered if I should have said more or done something different, for only a day later, she moved back into the travel trailer with that man. Shortly after that, the owner of the RV park had them removed because of the disruptions they were causing. I never saw her again.

The second greatest commandment the Lord gives us is to love our neighbor as ourselves. Wow! A "neighbor" can be someone who lives in proximity to where I live or it can be a fellow human being I come in contact with. Either way, I have found God usually places them in my life for a reason. For neighbors are like family, you don't get to pick who they are. Some become great friends, and they are the ones that are easy to love. Then some . . . are like small pieces of gritty sand that get stuck in your teeth, and they become a constant, annoying irritation. But Jesus said to love my neighbor, not just the one I like. Ouch! I hope I am not the only one challenged by this commandment. Please tell me I am not the only one challenged to love my neighbor.

Since a neighbor can pretty much be defined as anybody, Jesus wants us to love EVERYBODY. Yes, even our enemies (Matthew 5:44). That means there is no room for hate, nor is there time for hate. We are to love our fellow man where we live and across the globe. God wants every tongue, every tribe and every nation in heaven rejoicing before the Lamb of God (Revelation 7:9). We have a gracious God who does not want anyone to perish (2 Peter 3:9).

As Christians, I hope we share in the same desire as God to not want anyone to perish. It is imperative for us to spread the word of Jesus. The best way to do that is to love others well with our speech, actions and deeds.

John, Jesus' young disciple, understood this concept very well. I get tickled when I read John's writings in the Gospels. He would refer to himself as "the one Jesus loved, the beloved disciple". No one else in the scriptures refer to John that way...just him. That little tidbit just cracks me up. But the fact is: John knew who he was in Christ. He knew he was loved and that knowledge made it easier for him to love others—even in times of persecution.

Because John was secure in being loved by God, he was able to write the inspired word of 1 John 4:7-12 which states, *"Dear friends, let us love one another, for love comes from God. Everyone who loves has been born of God and knows God. Whoever does not love does not know God, because God is love. This is how God showed his love among us: He sent his one and only Son into the world that we might live through him. This is love: not that we loved God, but that he loved us and sent his Son as an atoning sacrifice for our sins. Dear friends, since God so loved us, we also ought to love one another. No one has ever seen God; but if we love one another, God lives in us and his love is made complete in us."*

How can we argue with John's writings? We simply can't. How are we to show God to the world? Love the world. We need to be an extension of His love, for God IS love. And as a born again believer, I have the power of the Holy Spirit living inside of me that gives me the capabilities to love the way God loves. I have to live by the Spirit.

John took this concept seriously and so should we. It has been written that near the end of his life, he constantly repeated the phrase, "Little children, love one another!" He did that because he believed it was the Lord's most important commandment.[8]

I have to confess, "I do not always love well and at times it can be very difficult for me." God places some difficult people in my life that I would like to just slap silly, but then I try to remind myself that God may be using this difficult person to work out some stuff in me. (Fun!?!) He may also be wanting me to minister to that person, and if I am acting ugly, I'm not going to be a lot of help to Him.

There is a prayer God has taught me to pray that really helps me love the unlovable. It is, "Lord, let me see this person as you see them." If I pray that prayer before I am around a person that aggravates me, I find God gives me the strength I need to be kind. It is not a fake kindness; I hate that. The gesture is sincere because it comes from God. God loves that person, and He wants me to love that person. God knows what makes that person the way they are, and God can open my spiritual eyes to see what He sees. He will reveal specifics about that person to me. When he gives me these revelations, my heart becomes tender and I discover how much easier it becomes to deal with this person; not just to deal with them, but to love them. That's God's way.

I have an abounding amount of the Father's love lavished on me for no good reason except for the fact that He loves me. So I ask myself, "Shouldn't some of that abounding love spill over onto others…it should; but is it?" Ohhh, sometimes God steps on my toes. Tough questions like this have to be asked of myself if I expect to mature as a Christian.

I know I don't have enough love of my own to spill over onto everybody that comes my way…I don't. I know I've mentioned it before, but it is imperative that I spend time with God in the morning and ask Him to fill me with His Spirit that I may flow in His love. My quiet time gets me off to a good start. When I am with Him first thing, I am reminded of how much He loves me and I love Him. I can take that with me and draw from that throughout the day. Sometimes, during the day, I will have to come back to Him and tell Him, "I need more of you right now. Help me love this person in a Godly way because I'm having a hard time here."

God is love and all perfect love comes from Him. God's ways are different from the world's ways. The world tells us to be lovers of ourselves, take care of ourselves first and then you will be more satisfied as a person and treat others better. It doesn't work. I've tried it and I just find myself in self-made messes—for self-motivated love always wants more self. It's selfish.

Self love given to self gets self-absorption. Self love given over to God is transformed into a Godly love that lends to a servant's heart. Self given to God is what allows us to live and love beyond ourselves—to do what we are not able to do in our own strength. We discover that loving others and serving them with humility gives us great fulfillment. To find ourselves, we must lose ourselves in God's love.

Loving others well does not mean we have to love blindly. We need to be smart, always kind, but loving with some discernment. God gives us discernment for a purpose. There may be some people that we come into contact with that for some reason are not good for us. In those instances, we need to be wise and listen to the Holy Spirit's direction. If the Holy Spirit is telling us, "You shouldn't be around this person," we need to listen. He is trying to protect us.

Proverbs 3:21-23 offers this jewel, "*My son, preserve sound judgment and discernment, do not let them out of your sight; they will be life for you, an ornament to grace your neck. Then you will go on your way in safety, and your foot will not stumble."*

We will be wise to use the discernment He gives us. It truly is a grace-given protection for us as believers. There can be several reasons why the Holy Spirit gives us warnings about a relationship.

One reason for a wise warning could be that person might lead us into a sin. How many times has a seemingly innocent friendship between co-workers turn into an affair that ends with devastating consequences. In the beginning, I'm pretty sure there was a warning inside them that said, "Walk away from this."

Or what about that friend your kid is hanging around with? If you don't have a good feeling about it, God is trying to tell you something. That kid could be trying to influence your child into drinking or doing drugs or being disrespectful. You need to exercise your judgment as a parent and say, "I don't think you need to be hanging around so-and-so." Your kids may not like it, but as a parent you have every right to do this. Parenting isn't for the weak.

My son has argued with me when I have picked up on something. Colton will say (usually with a tone), "How do you know that?" And my response is, "The Holy Spirit told me, so don't argue with me over this." Over time I am proven right, and I take the opportunity to remind Colton of my past warnings.

Another reason God may want you to use some boundaries with a person is because that person doesn't bring out the best in you. There may not be anything wrong with that person, but when the two of you get together it isn't honoring to

God. Maybe you start to gossip, or you always go shopping and spend money you don't need to spend.

There are lots of reasons to love smartly. Just remember to stay close to God and He will guide you in the best way to love others. Keep this key principle in mind: to be able to love my neighbor, I have to realize God loves me first. He demonstrates his own love for me in this, while I was still a sinner, Christ died for me. (Romans 5:8)

I was telling a friend of mine today, "This has been a hard chapter for me to write." She said, "I bet it's a long one!" We both laughed knowing my struggles.

There is so much to say on "Loving Thy Neighbor". There is so much to learn. I have come to the conclusion, "You can't go wrong if you love; so LOVE BIG!" As my favorite Sunday school teacher, Jim McKee, always says, "If you're going to err; err on the side of grace." So here is my advice to you *"Above all, love each other deeply, because love covers over a multitude of sins."* 1 Peter 4:8

9
Maintenance, Maintenance

Guarding our Hearts

*"This is what the LORD says: "Maintain justice
and do what is right, for my salvation is close at hand and my
righteousness will soon be revealed.
Blessed is the man who does this, the man who holds it fast,
who keeps the Sabbath without desecrating it,
and keeps his hand from doing any evil."*

Isaiah 56:1-2

Maintenance on the Cougar was constant. Jeff made a good
point when he would say, "This trailer was not made for
permanent living." There was continual upkeep of some kind
just to sustain our living conditions. And bless his heart, Jeff
was the upkeep man.

The first thing we noticed was a thirty gallon tank of propane did not provide our heating and cooking needs for long. When we camped in the trailer, a propane tank would last us for quite awhile. What a difference when we started living in it.

Since our spring that year was colder than usual, the propane seemed to be flying out of the tank. Jeff was a frequent guest at the propane dealership. He kept a steady pace of rotating the tanks out to keep us in heat. He would change the tanks out at least once a week during the cold spells.

The heater would be running inside to try to maintain warmth while the cold outside air pressed against the thin fiberglass shell. This would cause great condensation on the walls. We would wake up in the mornings to find the walls dripping with water and the windows foggy. I *do* think this was due to the poor insulation of the trailer and *not* due to the hot air produced by a boisterous family.

When the outside temperature started heating up, we turned to the air conditioner for relief. The cooling system had its limits as well. We had to be careful and not let it become too cool or the unit would freeze up. On the occasion that this would happen, we would have to turn off the air conditioner, and let it thaw out. The process could take some time—leaving us without any relief from the hot, dry Texas summer.

As the trailer started facing daily abuse, problems started showing up everywhere. Not only did the drawers go off track, but handles started to break. Door handles fell off and the screen door would not want to open. Mini-blinds would get stuck in an unwanted position. It was always something.

A couple of months after living in the trailer, the oven went out. Jeff called the RV dealership to ask what he would need to fix it. They suggested that it could be one of two things, and both required different parts to fix the problem. The parts were over a hundred dollars apiece, and the kicker was, the dealership wouldn't let you return unused parts. They were ours to keep. So after mulling that over, we decided we could do without the oven. It was June, and when I used the oven, the whole trailer would get hot anyway.

We might be able to do without an oven, but we did need a working refrigerator. We had noticed it was running all the time, but yet, our food didn't feel real cold—not a good sign. I am so thankful I am married to such a smart and handy man. After a thorough inspection, Jeff discovered that some insulation had fallen down and was blocking the vent for the refrigerator. Thank God the problem was easily solved!

Maintenance of a RV septic system is better left to the imagination. I'll just say it requires lots of chemicals. It was part of the trailer life, and I accepted that. But you know to top off our trailer experience, we had to have some toilet issues. I don't know about you, but toilet problems are my favorite—Not! And to wake up to them is the best!

In the wee hours of one particular morning, I put my feet down on the floor to feel wet carpet ooze between my toes. I turned on the light and discovered water was standing all about and flowing from the toilet. The part that shuts the water off after you flush had broken, and so the water continued to run and run and run. The water had filled the holding tank. After the tank was full, it filled the toilet, and then overflowed onto the floor and leaked down into the basement of the camper where we had lots of extras stored.

Jeff didn't have any problem replacing the broken piece. That was the easy part. Cleaning and airing out the camper took a little more effort. We were all glad to put that issue "behind" us (no pun intended). At least it didn't smell like burnt brussels sprouts!

Housekeeping was regular maintenance too. Dirt would cloud in the trailer like Pig Pen lived there. My friends would say with envy, "Well at least you don't have much house work to do." If they only had a clue! Sure it was a small space, but I was cleaning that small space constantly. The trailer was always dusty so I would have to clean windows and blinds and the furniture on a regular basis. I had to vacuum every day to pick-up the stuff the dog and kids tracked in on the nice blue carpet. Daily, I went through the routine of making the kid's beds out on the couch and on the dining table and then put it all up again for the next round. Even though I cleaned; it didn't smell like it. I tried every good smelling product I could find to keep the camper from having the special "eau de stinketh" aroma.

For the most part, maintaining the trailer consisted of treating minor things that weren't that big of a deal (except for the toilet, it was a big deal). But if we had left those things unattended, over time they would have caused the trailer to become nonfunctional—no longer able to serve its purpose.

Our spiritual lives are the same way. While our time here on earth is not permanent, we still have to consistently take care of ourselves. We have to maintain our walk with God, or we will be unable to fully serve our purpose in this life. *"For I know the plans I have for you," declares the* LORD, *"plans to prosper you and not to harm you, plans to give you hope and a future."* Jeremiah 29:11

God wants nothing more than for us to fulfill the dreams He has for our lives; but in order for us to walk into those dreams, we have to deliberately perform maintenance on our souls or we will deteriorate spiritually.

In the verse I picked for the start of this chapter, Isaiah 56:1 states, *"Maintain justice and do what is right…"* The word maintain comes from the Hebrew word *shamar* (shaw-mar) which means to guard or protect, preserve, keeper of self, or watchman.[9]

Another Hebrew word that is frequently used to express the idea of "guarding" something is *natsar*. Generally, *natsar* is a close synonym to the much more common verb, *shamar*, "to keep, tend."[10] Both Hebrew words are translated as guard in many verses in our Bibles.

I want to turn to the scriptures now and take a look at what it says about us guarding our lives.

David was a smart man and he knew *he* needed help in guarding *his* life. He turns to his Lord several times in the Psalms praying for God's help in this matter. Here are some examples:

> *"Guard my life and rescue me; let me not be put to shame, for I take refuge in you."* Psalm 25:20

> *"Guard my life, for I am devoted to you. You are my*

God; save your servant who trusts in you." Psalm 86:2

(I have to add that this next one is a prayer I should pray everyday to keep me out of trouble and on the road to righteousness!)

"Set a guard over my mouth, O LORD; keep watch over the door of my lips." Psalm 141:3

I told you David was a smart man. Well, his son Solomon had wisdom like no other, and he had a few things to say about guarding our lives as well. Here are some of Solomon's words of wisdom:

"Discretion will protect you, and understanding will guard you." Proverbs 2:1

"Hold on to instruction, do not let it go; guard it well, for it is your life." Proverbs 4:13

"Keep my commands and you will live; guard my teachings as the apple of your eye." Proverbs 7:2

"Above all else, guard your heart, for it is the wellspring of life." Proverbs 4:23

The words David and Solomon wrote stress the importance of keeping their lives in maintenance mode. I find it interesting that in each Psalm, David's request was for God to do the guarding; and in the Proverbs, Solomon was directing us to take active measure and do the guarding. We will be wise to apply both measures in our lives. Having a relationship with God and taking responsibility for our actions will help us keep our maintenance up.

Those God-breathed scriptures are words to pray and live by and are written to provide advice on how to protect ourselves from falling apart. We have to make wise decisions and become diligent in guarding what we bring into our lives and what we dish out.

So many of life's temptations seem innocent or minute at first, but they can turn into major problems if we don't guard against them.

We can easily justify a little white lie or gossip as no big deal. What about watching a movie or TV show that uses inappropriate language or is lacking any moral substance, and thinking it won't affect us in anyway. How about a few glances at something on the internet that is not appropriate. The list can go on and on.

We all have issues we struggle with. These small compromising issues, if left unchecked, can slowly blur the lines between right and wrong. Before you know it, we distance ourselves from God and find ourselves breaking down in need of some major soul repairs.

We are the guardians of our souls. We have the power to maintain our spiritual lives. We choose whether we want to maintain our lives or just let it fall apart from neglect. It is called free will. We are the ones that can find victory in being truthful; in not listening or spreading gossip. We can find victory in not going to the movies that compromise our beliefs or to turn the TV off when we can't find anything good to watch. We can find victory in keeping our internet time clean and family friendly. We have the choice and through the blood of Jesus as born again believers we have the power!

We have to be honest with ourselves and before God. We have to keep our lives in check. What is the best way to do that? Keep the time from when we sin, to the time we confess our sin—short. Go before God. Sincerely repent and tell Him where you struggle: where you blew it today and where you need help. He's listening and ready to give some divine intervention. It is daily maintenance. And it keeps Satan, the accuser, from getting a foothold on your sin and using it to wreak havoc.

A regular maintenance prayer to pray is Psalm 139:23-24. *"Search me, O God, and know my heart; test me and know my anxious thoughts. See if there is any offensive way in me, and lead me in the way everlasting."* Trust me; there is always something to work on. Maintenance takes effort on our part. I've never seen any maintenance happen without a little elbow grease. But the rewards of a kept-up, victorious walk with God are well worth it. The benefit is we will be able to function to the fullest of God's divine purpose in our lives.

No matter how much maintenance went into the travel trailer, it still depreciated in value. That is just the way the system works. However, unlike the travel trailer, we don't have to depreciate in value. In God's kingdom, with a little righteous maintenance, we can become better than we were. We can *appreciate* in value. That is *the way* God's maintenance system works. Awesome.

10

A Place to Call Home

Heaven's Waiting

"Do not let your hearts be troubled. Trust in God; trust also in me.
In my Father's house are many rooms; if it were not so, I would have told you. I am going there to prepare a place for you.
And if I go and prepare a place for you, I will come back and take you to be with me that you also may be where I am.
You know the way to the place where I am going."

John 14:1-4

We had patiently waited for the house to be complete before we started moving in. Several people that had been through the building process advised us, "Do not rush in before you finish all the details; for if you do, the details never seem to get done. Complete the work." We thought that was good counsel; therefore, we made sure every bit of trim was painted and every door knob on before we put a stick of furniture in the new house.

The day finally came! The day the home was finished, over, done, over and done with (well, you get the idea), and we were ready to move in. December 6, 2005 was moving day. What a glorious day that was.

I can't begin to explain the sense of accomplishment we felt in being able to bring the furniture and all our belongings through the freshly painted front door. The focus of our time and energy for nine months was coming to an end.

The kids now had their own bedrooms and bathrooms, and Jeff and I had a beautiful master bedroom and bath retreat. I thought all would be joyful over our newly acquired surroundings, but I was wrong.

Some anxiety had set in, especially among the kids. We had grown accustomed to our tiny living quarters and became content with our trailer living; even though, there was a much nicer, safer, bigger home awaiting us just a few feet away—one that we had been preparing for daily.

While we knew the Cougar *was not* our permanent home, we had gotten comfortable in our familiar surroundings and felt the security of everybody being close together. The uncertainty of crossing over to something different overshadowed the excitement of entering into our permanent residence.

As creatures of habit, we looked at our new home, and it seemed like our bedrooms were worlds apart. We feared the closeness we shared would be lost. We were holding on to what we knew despite the fact that what was waiting for us would far surpass our current dwellings.

Oh, but once we moved in, the insecurity we felt faded away with long hot showers and restful slumber on fluffy mattresses and dinners without breakers going off. It didn't take long for the new house to become our new home.

I think our earthly lives can be reflected in our experience of making the transition from the camper to our new home. We were so accustomed to our camper; we were hesitant to move into the better place that was before us. As Christians, we can get so focused on our life here on earth as we know it. We forget it is temporary and our eternal life is the forever one—the one that will last.

Paul reminds us of this in 2 Corinthians 4:16-18, *"Therefore we do not lose heart. Though outwardly we are wasting away, yet inwardly we are being renewed day by day. For our light and momentary troubles are achieving for us an eternal glory that far outweighs them all. So we fix our eyes not on what is seen, but on what is unseen. For what is seen is temporary, but what is unseen is eternal."*

That scripture speaks to me. Fix your eyes on what is unseen for it is eternal. I never get tired of the hope God gives us through His word. Hope of eternity is a promise from God.

As I get older (not that I am old), the hope of eternity gives great meaning to my life's journey. It means that someday all wrongs will be made right. It means there is more to life than this world and what it has to offer. It means saying good-bye to friends and loved ones that have died is only temporary for those that know the Lord. It means I will spend eternity in the presence of God. Wow.

Let's take a deeper look into what it means to have eternity waiting for us.

First, all wrongs will be made right. He sees every injustice that happens to you and me, His precious children. While we are here on earth, God expects us to forgive those who have wronged us just as Jesus has forgiven us. Forgiving frees us from those who hurts us and allows God to deal with them. He sees the true heart of people. We have to trust Him in this. God is just and vengeance is His to take—not ours. In 2 Thessalonians 1:6-7 Paul tells us, *"God is just: He will pay back trouble to those who trouble you and give relief to you who are troubled, and to us as well. This will happen when the Lord Jesus is revealed from heaven in blazing fire with his powerful angels."*

When Jesus returns, God will judge all mankind. Only those written in the Lamb's book of life spend eternity with Him, and those that have rejected Jesus will spend eternity in hell.

When we enter heaven, there will be no more sorrow or tears; only joy and peace will fill our hearts. Jealousy and hate will be gone and perfect love will rule for eternity. Nothing impure will ever enter in. Satan is vanquished and no enemy will be found in our presence.

Second, a perfect home is waiting for us on the other side of this realm. We don't have to live our lives as if this is all there is—chasing after things that won't matter in the long run. The most beautiful things we seek here on earth will be like rubbish compared to the wonders of heaven. As Billy Graham says, "I've never seen a U-Haul following a hurst."

We can look forward to streets made of pure gold, crystal waters flowing, precious stones laid as the foundation of the city, gates made of pearl, and light, why the Lord God will be our light. Revelation shows us that heaven promises to be a stunning place and the only things we will want to bring with us are other people (and a pet or two).

Third, the biggest, grandest family reunion EVER waits for us on the other side. There to greet us, when we arrive at our final destination, will be our loved ones we had to say goodbye to here on earth and some relatives we have never met. I have grandparents I never knew this side of heaven. I'll get to see them someday. And I can't wait to meet my heroes of the faith. Can you imagine talking face to face with King David and Joseph? What about Mary? Don't you want to ask her what it was like to raise Jesus? I'm telling you, it is going to be a grand reunion, and up there, we are all family. Do you think we get matching family reunion t-shirts? I'm just asking.

For a season, God seemed to call a lot of people home. In a matter of a few months, people I knew and people I loved, were gone. Jeff's grandfather died at the age of 93. One of Colton's friends lost his mother after a long battle with cancer. She was 37. The day of her funeral, my mother died from pancreatic cancer. My mom was two days shy of her 80th birthday. A few weeks later, a friend of mine lost her daughter in a skiing accident. She was 10. Too much death. Too many funerals. For a time there, it was almost more than I could bear.

This side of heaven we may not understand why our loved ones have to leave us when they do; even though, as believers, we know we will get to be reunited with them again. It still hurts. We miss them. Death comes to everyone's door. Until Jesus' triumphant return, we all will face death. But death doesn't have the final say—Jesus does! I need to know that.

And saving the best for last, the hope of eternity means being in the full presence of the Holy Trinity—the Father, Son and Holy Spirit. I know that is so much more than we can even imagine. I can't even begin to know what that must be like. For those in the Bible that got a glimpse of the Glory, they immediately knew their unworthiness and were fully aware of the Holiness they saw. Isaiah, Ezekiel and John all fell face down when they saw visions of the LORD. And they expressed that mere words could not do justice to what they saw. They heard a voice like rushing water, saw hair as white as snow and looked upon eyes blazing—a God worthy of our worship. Can you imagine getting to have an intimate face to face conversation with Jesus? Ponder that for awhile.

After my mom passed away, I had a dream where I was by her side. I said to her, "I'm sorry. We should have sought out more alternatives for you when we found out you had cancer. You might have gotten to be with us a little longer." But in my dream, my mom said, "Don't be sorry; it is more than we ever imagined."

Heaven is more than we can ever imagine—so much more.

My heart goes out to those who don't put their hope in the Lord. For what hope do they have when they lose a loved one, or when they face death themselves. Where is their hope? They won't find it in false religions, in money, power or fame. No, the only place they will find hope is in a place I call home—where I am not an alien, but a welcomed child and heir with Jesus Christ.

Come home with me. I pray that you have asked Jesus to be your Lord and Savior just as I did when I was ten years old at the First Baptist Church of Vega, Texas. I was baptized into the kingdom with my brothers and my best friend, DeeDee. God gives us the gift of eternity through Jesus; all we have to do is receive it.

If we put our lives in God's hands, our time here on earth will not be for naught. Live the life of faith. It will have purpose and meaning. For we are aliens of this land, passing through; our home awaits us in heaven. Sometimes we hold on to what is familiar to us. Instead, we should live a life of godly abandonment knowing that what awaits us is far beyond what we have here.

My prayer for you and me is this, *"Dear friends, I urge you, as aliens and strangers in the world, to abstain from sinful desires, which war against your soul. Live such good lives among the pagans that, though they accuse you of doing wrong, they may see your good deeds and glorify God on the day he visits us."* 1 Peter 2:11-12

I want to live my life as if I am building up my home in heaven where moth and rust won't destroy it and thieves won't steal from it. (Matthew 6:19-20) Let me be a part of God's house where Ephesians 2:19-22 is my reality, *"You are no longer foreigners and aliens, but fellow citizens with God's people and members of God's household, built on the foundation of the apostles and prophets, with Christ Jesus himself as the chief cornerstone. In him the whole building is joined together and rises to become a holy temple in the Lord. And in him you too are being built together to become a dwelling in which God lives by his Spirit."*

Aahh…now that's a place to call home.

Conclusion

I wonder if the Cougar was lonely once we were gone. We did visit her from time to time after we moved out, but it was never the same. Things were just different. The cabinets were bare, the closet actually had some empty hangers and those pesky drawers were begging to be stuffed. We didn't need her in the way we once did. We had moved on and so go our lives.

The adventure had come to an end, but our lives are richer because of those four fiberglass walls and the 224 square feet inside them. My family shared an experience we will not soon forget. I have the Cougar to thank for that.

Life's a journey for all of us—full of one adventure after another. And each adventure we take, changes us somehow. The adventures can be set against the back drops of magnificent mountain tops and refreshing streams, or they can be found in long stretches of dry harsh dessert and deep valleys. None are ever alike. There may even be a few detours and roadblocks thrown in along the way. We may even get ourselves lost a time or two, but we can get back on track if we ask God for directions. (Yes, men it is okay to ask for directions.)

The key to safe traveling is to let God be our guide. Along with Him, Jesus provides the way, and with them, comes our map which is the Word of God and our compass which is the Holy Spirit living inside of each believer. That is the perfect navigational system for our lives. If we follow the course God lays out for us, we can rest assure our lives will have meaning and purpose. He may not lead us where we always want to go, but it will always be where we need to be. And His timing will be perfect for each new trail we set off on. And our Lord, in His great wisdom, will reveal to us spiritual lessons in each adventure as long as we keep our eyes on Him and the map.

In every aspect of my life's journey, I grow closer to Him and His teachings—my life lessons. Some lessons come wrapped as wonderful gifts from above. Some lessons come through a gentle nudge or revelation, and sometimes I get the lessons when I have had my feet knocked out from under me and I am lying face down in desperation.

Oh, but my God is faithful. He sees me through. I have laughed and I have cried as I have journeyed with my Jesus. And He has been with me every step of the way even in those times when I felt like no one was there.

As we travel up and down life's highway, it helps to remember the adventure leads us straight to Jesus. When you get tired and weary and don't want to go any further, look up, for you are traveling on your way to glory. Isaiah 35:8-10 reminds us of that. The title above this chapter in my Bible reads *Joy of the Redeemed*. Take in these precious words, *"A highway will be there; it will be called the Way of Holiness. The unclean will not journey on it; it will be for those who walk in that Way; wicked fools will not go about on it. No lion will be there, nor will any ferocious beast get up on it; they will not be found there. But only the redeemed will walk there, and the ransomed of the LORD will return. They will enter Zion with singing; everlasting joy will crown their heads. Gladness and joy will overtake them, and sorrow and sighing will flee away."*

The Way of Holiness, now that is a road I want to travel on. With or without wheels!

Appendix
The Book Ministry

It is my prayer that this book ministers to those who read it. Writing it has been a labor of love. Only in God's sovereign design would He create this opportunity for me—to write a book of all things.

For years my mother had a book ministry. On any given day the trunk of her car would be full of books like: *God's Calling, Prayers That Avail Much, Woman Thou Art Loosed! Holy Bible* or *Tough-Minded Faith for Tender-Hearted People.* She would take these books and many others and give them away to anyone God placed on her heart. Whether she knew the person or not was irrelevant. She knew God knew them and their needs—that's all that mattered to her.

Since Mom is no longer with us, I can't help but think that with the writing of this book, Mom's book ministry lives on in some way.

My mother was diagnosed with pancreatic cancer on September 17, 2008. By the time the doctors found it, there really wasn't anything the doctors could do for her. Her name was Martha and she loved the Lord with all her heart (I imagine her love for Him now is beyond our worldly knowledge as she is in Jesus' presence), and she had a great faith. Her hope was in Him.

When the doctors discovered Mom's cancer, she was having surgery on her stomach. The surgery was successful. But the next day she couldn't breathe, and they intubated her. She was moved to ICU and there she lay on a respirator.

We knew this wasn't what she wanted and she was irritated that she couldn't communicate with us. I thought of giving her a tablet and a pen because she had some things to say, and she seemed pretty adamant about it. She started writing, and we started deciphering. I felt like we were in charades. Mom's handwriting was shaky because her hands were strapped down so she wouldn't pull out the respirator, and her spelling left something to be desired.

In crisis she knew where her foundation was. She was standing on the solid Rock. This was just one more time to see God work a miracle in her life. She had seen Him do it before, and she was ready for Him to do it again. All the years of a true relationship, reading the Bible and listening to gospel music gave her strength to fight.

The ICU nurses were gracious enough to let us honor her request to plug in a CD player and get that Tennessee Ernie Ford music going. She wanted her Joyce Meyer's book full of healing scriptures, her T. D. Jakes Bible, and she wanted certain people called to pray for her (ones that believed in miraculous healing). We took our marching orders as a mission from God and left until our next visiting time.

While we were away, Mom had been doing some talking with God because the next time we went in for a visit; she had some more orders for us. She wrote that God told her she was to have a healing service in her room, and she had two certain men in mind to do it.

I looked at my brother and I said, "I don't know what I am going to do. I have already talked to the wife of one of them this morning, and they are leaving for a Texas Tech football game this afternoon." I wanted to do whatever I could, but I didn't know how I was going to pull this off. Well, I wasn't the one that was supposed to be doing anything. God was. He had it handled.

Before our visiting hour was up, guess who walked in. You got it! The exact two men my mom had believed would pray for her healing. God had told them to get up there, and they were obedient. They prayed healing over my mom and sang over her.

I have to say, "These aren't quiet guys. That whole unit heard the praises of the saints." Who knows what kind of healing went on in the lives of the people around? We had a church service! The power of the Holy Spirit was there in that little hospital room. And once again, the Lord showed us favor with the nurses because they didn't shoo us out of there even if we went forty minutes past the visiting hour.

Martha loved it! She believed she was healed. Immediately, her numbers started improving and the respirator was off the next morning, and in just a few days she was ready to leave the hospital. The whole time she was praising her Healer to anyone who would listen.

God was so good to her. Mom never was in any pain in the following months, and we had a wonderful Thanksgiving with the entire family at her house. She was happy.

The Saturday after Thanksgiving, some of the kids and grandkids decorated her house for her favorite season— Christmas. We thought we were being sneaky by not putting out *every* Nativity scene and decoration; but as soon as we left, Dad said, "She went and found the missing decorations and set them out."

The following week, Mom went downhill fast. Jaundice started showing on her skin and a week from our decorating extravaganza she was gone. Wearing her best Christmas attire and her favorite red hat, she went to see Jesus in high fashion. Martha was ready to spend Christmas in heaven.

She didn't want to leave her family. She was still concerned about her grandkids, and she was hoping for one of her grandchildren to make her a great-grandmother. But a friend of mine said, "I think Martha got a glimpse of Jesus, and she couldn't resist going home to be with Him."

Mom died December 6, 2008. She moved into her heavenly home exactly three years after I had moved into my earthly home.

Since Mom has been gone, I continue to see the prayers of a righteous person availing much. (James 5:16) By no means was my mother a perfect woman. She had her faults and could drive me crazy. But her love of the Lord was real. She had a daily relationship with Jesus. She believed in the power of prayer, and she shared her love of the Lord with others by giving away Bibles and Christian books.

God used her in spite of her imperfections, just like He uses me and every other person that calls Him Lord of their lives.

I believe I have the promise from God's word that He will continue a good work through Mom's life and others that loved the Lord and left us before we were ready for them to go. They were still living by faith when they died just like the heroes of faith in Hebrews 11. Just read the inspiring word of Hebrews 11:13-16, *"All these people were still living by faith when they died. They did not receive the things promised; they only saw them and welcomed them from a distance. And they admitted that they were aliens and strangers on earth. People who say such things show that they are looking for a country of their own. If they had been thinking of the country they had left, they would have had opportunity to return. Instead, they were longing for a better country — a heavenly one. Therefore God is not ashamed to be called their God, for he has prepared a city for them."* I just love those verses. They give me such comfort.

Mom and others may not have seen all the things promised to them when they died, but I think God will continue working it out because of Philippians 1:3-6. It says, *"I thank my God every time I remember you. In all my prayers for all of you, I always pray with joy because of your partnership in the gospel from the first day until now, being confident of this, that he who began a good work in you will carry it on to completion until the day of Christ Jesus."*

God will continue to use the books Mom gave away to minister to people. He will remember her prayers for her grandchildren. He will continue to work her faith out here on earth.

If Mom were alive today, I know her trunk would be full of *Goin' On A Road Trip Without Any Wheels*. She never got to read my book. She was gone before I had a chance to finish the first draft of my manuscript. I'm hoping the Lord will give her a heavenly copy. Who knows…maybe she is busy passing around copies in heaven. I wouldn't put it past her.

Endnotes

Chapter 5

1 Holman Illustrated Bible Dictionary Copyright 2003 by Holman Bible Publishers. Nashville, Tennessee. All rights reserved. Page 1370

2 Barnes' Notes, Electronic Database Copyright © 1997, 2003 by Biblesoft, Inc. All rights reserved.

Chapter 6

3 Revised Edition of: American Heritage dictionary of the English language. New college edition. c1976

Chapter 7

4 http://www.srh.noaa.gov/ama/climate/2007wxreview.htm

5 http://www.srh.noaa.gov/ama/climate/2007wxreview.htm
6 http://www.srh.noaa.gov/ama/climate/2007wxreview.htm

7 http://en.wikipedia.org/wiki/How_Great_Thou_Art

(hymn)

Chapter 8

8 http://www.allaboutjesuschrist.org/history-of-john-the-disciple-of-jesus-faq.htm

Chapter 9

9 Biblesoft's New Exhaustive Strong's Numbers and Concordance with Expanded Greek-Hebrew Dictionary. Copyright © 1994, 2003 Biblesoft, Inc. and International Bible Translators, Inc.

10 Vine's Expository Dictionary of Biblical Words, Copyright © 1985, Thomas Nelson Publishers.